4/15/09

D0570068

Confetti Cakes

for kids

Confetti Cakes
for kids

DELIGHTFUL **COOKIES, CAKES,** AND **CUPCAKES**
FROM NEW YORK CITY'S FAMED BAKERY

Elisa Strauss
with CHRISTIE MATHESON

PHOTOGRAPHS BY BEN FINK

1837

Little, Brown and Company
NEW YORK • BOSTON • LONDON

Little, Brown and Company
Hachette Book Group USA
237 Park Avenue, New York, NY 10017
Visit our Web site at www.HachetteBookGroupUSA.com

First Edition: October 2008

Little, Brown and Company is a division of Hachette Book Group USA, Inc.
The Little, Brown name and logo are trademarks of Hachette Book Group
USA, Inc.

Library of Congress Cataloging-in-Publication Data
Strauss, Elisa.
    Confetti Cakes for kids: delightful cookies, cakes, and cupcakes from New
York City's famed bakery / Elisa Strauss ; with Christie Matheson. — 1st ed.
            p. cm.
    Includes index.
    ISBN 978-0-316-11829-3
    1. Cake decorating. 2. Cake. 3. Confetti Cakes (Bakery)
I. Matheson, Christie. II. Title.
    TX771.2.S774 2008
    641.8'653 — dc22   2007042880

10 9 8 7 6 5 4 3 2 1

Printed in China

Designed by Empire Design Studio

To my loving grandparents,
the late Pearl and Philip Gustin, and Shirley and Carl Strauss
They taught me the importance of family from the moment I was born
and never let a milestone in my life pass uncelebrated.
From each of them, I received the gifts of love, creativity, and
continuous encouragement. This one girl is fortunate enough to
have had *four* amazing grandparents in her life.

Contents

Introduction

. . .

When I look back on my childhood,
one thing that always sticks out in my memory
are the cakes people made for me.
They were each distinctive for the occasion
and tasted simply delicious.
And whatever the cause for celebration,
I knew someone had done something special for me.

. . .

I remember one that my mom made in the shape of a little duck. She covered it in yellow buttercream and used a jellybean for the eye! Another time my brother and I worked together to make a cake that resembled Mickey Mouse. And when I was older I had a safari-themed party with an animal kingdom–inspired cake. It was eye-opening to realize that cakes could go beyond basic round or square shapes with plain frosting, and that's part of what inspired me to become a pastry chef and to run Confetti Cakes, my bakery in New York City. I wanted to design cakes that would make people feel special and create lasting memories.

Kids get so excited when they see one of our cakes — especially if it's a cake made just for them. They marvel at the mere sight of it, and can't wait to have a bite. Confetti Cakes receives countless requests for cakes to commemorate different occasions in kids' lives: birthdays (from the first to the eighteenth), graduations (from preschool through college), bar and bat mitzvahs, holidays, and more. And sometimes — I love it when we do this — we are asked to make cakes to celebrate the little things in life, like the first day of school or a slumber party.

We have many clients who come back to us every year and ask us to create a special birthday cake for their child's party. And many of these kids get quite involved in "designing" their cakes, which

is wonderful. The little ones have strong opinions (if you are a parent, this won't surprise you) about what the cake should look and taste like; after all, they want their friends to be thrilled when they see it and take a bite.

We've made kids' cakes inspired by everything from the memory of a favorite stuffed animal to a child's school backpack to wonderful children's books. My favorite confections for kids, including versions of many of our most popular cakes and cakes that I've made on television, are featured in this book. There are 24 fantastic projects — cookies, cupcakes, mini cakes, and large cakes — that are guaranteed to make any event memorable. We've also included more than 20 recipes for making a variety of flavored cakes, cookies, frostings, and fillings that are as delicious as the cakes are beautiful. Because no matter what a cake looks like, it's only fun when it tastes incredible.

It's even more fun when kids are involved in the process of baking and decorating the cake — and there are many opportunities for kids to help with the cakes in this book. They can choose their favorite flavors and fillings, knead dough, mix colors, sprinkle sanding sugar, sift flour and cocoa, stir in ingredients, help think of designs, and hopefully help clean up — or just watch you work and enjoy spending time in the kitchen. Because baking and decorating involve math, science, and plenty of creativity, this is sure to be a learning experience you can share together.

Throughout the book are detailed instructions and illustrations to guide you through every aspect of these projects and photos to inspire your work in the kitchen. We also offer insider tips gleaned from my hundreds upon hundreds of hours spent making cakes for kids. Whether you prepare the simplest cookies or the most elaborate sculpted cake, kids of all ages will adore the results.

Cake Basics

Here are descriptions of the
equipment, decorating tools, decorations,
and baking terms mentioned
frequently in this book. If you like to bake
and decorate cakes, knowing
these terms and having the right equipment
and tools in your kitchen will
make the process much easier and more fun!

Equipment

Don't worry if your kitchen isn't already stocked with every item on this list — but you may want to add certain pieces to your collection as you work on specific projects in this book. If you prepare cakes often, you will use them again and again. (Refer to the photograph on the next page.)

1. Scale: If you can, use a scale instead of measuring cups to measure dry ingredients. A scale provides precise measurements, which helps recipes come out exactly right. The amount of ingredients in measuring cups may vary depending on how you spoon them in, and it's easy to lose count when you need many cups of an ingredient. Using a scale helps the process go more quickly, and the cleanup, too — it cuts down on spilling.

2. Fondant smoothers: These paddles help cake decorators of all levels create a smooth, bump- and ripple-free fondant surface. We use them to smooth fondant after we've placed it on a cake. They are also useful for centering finished cakes on bases or on top of other tiers of cake without leaving any finger marks.

3. Standing mixer: Using a heavy-duty standing mixer rather than a handheld mixer can help you achieve better, more consistent results when baking cakes. It also makes dealing with thick cookie dough and icing much easier.

4. Tape measure: This comes in handy for measuring the curved surfaces of cakes and sugar decorations.

5. Wooden rolling pin: Use this for rolling out sheets of cookie dough and large pieces of fondant. Many bakers use a metal or marble rolling pin with handles; we prefer wood.

6. Serrated knives: These knives are essential for cutting cakes without compressing them the way smooth-bladed knives do. A large serrated knife is necessary for splitting layers of cake, and a smaller version helps you carve and sculpt with precision.

7. Long metal ruler: An 18-inch ruler can guide you in cutting cake and measuring cake layers, cake boards, and the overall height of a cake. It is the perfect tool for measuring rolled fondant. Choose metal over plastic or wood because it's more durable and less likely to be cut or dented, so it will always have a perfectly straight edge.

8. Cake drum: For a lighter cake, you can buy a premade foil-covered base and cover it with fondant, fabric, paper, or Royal Icing. For heavier cakes (cakes with more than three tiers) we suggest making the base out of wood. Usually a local hardware store can cut it for you.

9. Paring knife: Small, sharp, and easy to handle, this knife has a smooth blade good for cutting fondant, gum paste, and marzipan, trimming fondant-covered cakes, and creating straight edges.

10. Rubber spatula: This utensil is useful for scraping batter from a bowl, filling pastry bags, and transferring filling from a bowl to a cake pan.

11. Cardboard cake board: Support each tier of cake with at least one of these boards underneath it — tiers of 6 inches or more need at least two. This allows you to move cakes easily and lift them after they are covered in fondant. A tier with a cardboard cake board underneath can also be glued directly to a cake base or placed on top of dowels. Cardboard cake boards should be exactly the same size or slightly smaller than the tiers of cake they are supporting. If you don't have cardboard, you can use foam core to make a cake base.

12. Cupcake wrappers: Place cupcake wrappers directly into cupcake tins and pour cake batter into them; they make handling individual cupcakes easier and they come in a variety of fun colors, shapes, and sizes.

13. *Large piping tip:* A pastry bag fitted with a large piping tip is a good tool to use to place filling between layers of cake — by piping rather than spreading with a spatula you will achieve uniform height over the entire layer. We also use the points of these tips for cutting out polka dots and other round sugar decorations.

14. *Bench scraper:* By removing cornstarch and other ingredients from your work table, you can keep a clean work surface at all times with this tool. You can also use its metal edge to cut fondant and gum paste into pieces, and to push Royal Icing from the back of a pastry bag up to the front tip in order to eliminate bubbles.

15. *Measuring spoons:* Use these to measure ingredients in small increments: ⅛ teaspoon, ¼ teaspoon, ½ teaspoon, 1 teaspoon, and 1 tablespoon. Level off ingredients before adding them to a recipe.

16. *Measuring cups:* Spoon ingredients into the cups with a tablespoon and level off the top with a straight edge to make sure your measurements are as accurate as possible.

17. *Small offset spatula:* Similar to a palette knife, but wider and thicker, this tool is convenient for transferring cookies and cakes, frosting cupcakes, spreading icings and preserves, crumb coating cakes, and mixing colors of Royal Icing.

18. *Long offset spatula:* This tool can cover more surface area than the smaller version when you are frosting large cakes, and works well for moving large layers of cake.

NOT PICTURED:

Cake pans: Heavyweight metal pans generally produce the best baking results — try to avoid pans that feel light and flexible. Even if you use nonstick pans, line them with parchment paper when baking. For silicone pans, follow the manufacturer's directions — usually you just need to brush them with a thin layer of butter and you don't need parchment paper.

Dry pastry brush: Reserve a wide, flat brush of about 2 to 5 inches in width to brush away cornstarch when you're rolling out fondant.

Double boiler: Rather than melting chocolate in a pot directly over a heat source, use either a double boiler or a heatproof bowl set over a pot of simmering water.

Foam core: You've probably seen this white craft board with a waxy surface and a layer of foam in the middle used to mount posters, but it also works as a cake base or a cake board to support individual tiers of cake. It's stronger than cardboard, and the surface material repels moisture and grease better. You can cut it easily with an X-acto knife.

Handsaw: We use a small handsaw to cut wooden dowels, because it's much easier to use than a serrated knife, which could become dull if you cut wood too often.

Pasta machine: Though this machine is traditionally used to shape pasta dough into thin sheets, cake decorators use it to cut down on the elbow grease needed to achieve the thickness of gum paste or fondant they desire. Start with a thicker setting and work towards thinner until you have the thickness you need to cut out your decorations. (See page 52.)

Pencil sharpener: Sharpen the ends of wooden dowels before you insert them into a cake.

Plastic and wooden dowels: **Never** use straws to dowel a cake — they can easily bend and crack and your cake could collapse. Use plastic dowels for larger tiers and skinnier wooden dowels when there's not as much room.

Sieve: It's easier to sift your dry ingredients all at once if you use a large, flat-bottomed, round sieve that you can hold with two hands, one on each side. If you don't have a sieve, you can use a sifter.

Turntable: A turntable allows you to turn your cake without touching it, which is very helpful when you're icing and decorating. Use a sturdy metal turntable, since plastic ones can be flimsy and may tip or break. If you don't have a turntable, improvise by turning over a heavy, round cake pan and place your cake on top of that.

Wet pastry brush: Keep a small flat brush, about 1 to 3 inches wide, to coat cake pans with butter and brush simple syrup onto cake layers. Wash thoroughly between uses.

Wooden mallet or hammer: Use to help you "hammer" dowels (gently!) through cake layers.

Wooden skewers: To determine the height of your cake before cutting dowels, stick a skewer into the middle of a cake, mark the height of the top of the cake on the skewer, and pull it out. Skewers can also lend support to sugar decorations.

Decorating Tools

We couldn't create the beautiful, detailed decorations that adorn our cakes without tools to help us. These are many of the instruments we rely on daily. (Refer to the photograph on the next page.)

1. Plastic mat: A mat intended for food use — or any smooth placemat — is great for rolling out small quantities of fondant or gum paste. Lay a damp paper towel flat underneath the mat to keep it from sliding while you roll. We use the disposable mats found in grocery stores; you can reuse them again and again.

2. Drafting triangle: Cake designers use this to create right angles, vertical and diagonal lines, and quilted patterns. Its narrow point slides easily into small spaces and can serve as a guideline.

3. Clay gun: By inserting different disks (three are shown) into the clay gun, you can push softened fondant, gum paste, or marzipan into many different shapes and sizes for all sorts of decorations. Marzipan and softened gum paste are the best materials for making long strings and other elongated shapes. You can find clay guns at most arts and crafts shops.

4. Stitching tool: Also called a tracing wheel, this device renders the look of actual stitching on fondant and gum paste.

5. Gum paste tools: The veining tool, dog-bone tool, and ball tool can emboss and help to sculpt fondant, gum paste, and marzipan decorations. You can also use them to shape flower petals and leaves, and to create hollow centers in sugar decorations.

6. Plastic blossom cutters: These plastic cutters don't rust, are easy to clean, cut precise little shapes, and can also be used for embossing.

7. Pastry bag: A pastry bag holds icing or filling when you need to pipe designs onto a cookie or cake or create a swirl of frosting on cupcakes. We prefer to use disposable plastic bags, which make cleanup easy and keep your buttercream and ganache (which contain fats) separate from your Royal Icing (which has no fat). Cloth bags are tougher on your hands and harder to clean.

8. Pastry tips: These are necessary for piping designs. Different sizes give different piping effects. Each size is assigned a number (such as #10 or #806). Always wash and dry pastry tips thoroughly so they don't rust.

9. Cookie cutters: Use metal or plastic cutters to get perfect shapes from cookie dough, rolled fondant, and gum paste.

10. Leaf cutters: These metal cutters form the general shape of leaves for plant or flower decorations; after cutting you can shape them further with gum-paste tools, a mold, or your hand.

11. Small metal ruler: Look for a 12-inch metal ruler (as opposed to wood or plastic, which can get cut or dented) with no backing for measuring and cutting gum paste.

12. Paintbrushes: Paint and dust cookies, cupcakes, and cakes using good quality brushes. Use small brushes for fine details and larger brushes for dry dusting sugar decorations. For the tiny details, use a brush with bristles that come together to form a point.

13. Palette knife: This tool slides easily under thinly rolled gum paste or fondant so you can pick it up; you can also use it to get under a cookie or cake base that's still drying.

14. **Plastic rolling pin:** The smooth surface of this small rolling pin makes it ideal for rolling small amounts of fondant and gum paste on a plastic mat.

15. **Scissors:** Keep a pair of sharp scissors around for cutting out templates and patterns and trimming the edges of cake boards.

16. **Scalpel:** The very fine, sharp blade on a scalpel can cut tiny decoration details with great precision. Just be careful! You can find scalpels at medical supply stores.

17. **X-acto knife:** Use this tool's thin, sharp blade to create templates and sugar decorations, and to cut cardboard and foam core into the shape you need.

NOT PICTURED:

Cloth-covered wires: We use these to make loop bows (page 55) and sometimes to add dimension to sugar flowers. This flexible metal wire comes in different weights, from #18 gauge (the heaviest) to #28 gauge (the lightest). For heavier decorations, be sure to use stronger wire.

Egg cartons: Recycle your egg cartons! Make sure they're clean and use the compartments for drying fondant and gum paste decorations.

Lollipop sticks: These paper-covered sticks are used to support cookies and sugar decorations. You can find them at craft and cake decorating stores in different sizes.

Tweezers: We use tweezers when we need to place very small and delicate decorations — such as dragées — gently and carefully.

Decorations

The products pictured here help us add color, sparkle, and shine to our cakes.

1. **Petal dust:** Also known as powdered food coloring, this comes in many colors and is used to decorate dried sugar decorations. Apply it dry with a brush, or mix it with lemon extract to form a liquid paint. It's shown here in large (18-gram) and small (4-gram) containers.

2. **Luster dust:** When you want sparkle on your cake, use this powder to add shine. You can apply it dry, but it's usually mixed with lemon extract and painted directly on cakes or sugar decorations.

3. **Metallic powder:** This works like luster dust, and it gives the look of real metal.

4. **Lemon extract:** The pure form of lemon extract has a high concentration of alcohol and evaporates quickly, so it's a good mixing agent to use for painting with petal and luster dusts. It's shown here in a squeeze bottle.

5. **Squeeze bottle:** Dispense small quantities of liquid easily from these containers.

6. **Edible pearls:** Formed from gum paste, edible pearls are hardened in the shape of a pearl and then mixed with super pearl luster dust. You can buy pre-pared edible pearls or make them yourself.

7. **Rock candy:** To simulate the look of crystals with an edible element, add rock candy to frosted cupcakes or cakes.

8. **Nonpareils:** These little candies add a touch of retro color to cookies and cupcakes.

9. **Sanding sugar:** This fine sugar, available in a rainbow of colors, adds sparkly texture to cookies and the tops of cupcakes.

10. **Edible glitter:** This edible decoration works just like real glitter — you shake it on and discard the excess.

11. **Dragées:** Nothing else provides the same metallic look as dragées, so we do use them — but because they don't have great flavor or texture, we use them sparingly.

12. **Vodka:** The high alcohol concentration in vodka makes it ideal for removing unwanted marks on your cakes. It evaporates quickly and leaves no taste behind. It's also the liquid component to mix with food coloring gels to form paints.

13. **Cotton swabs:** Dip a swab into a small amount of vodka and rub it gently on the surface of cakes to remove any unwanted marks. Don't worry: It will evaporate and will not leave behind any alcohol flavor.

14. **Food markers:** Write directly on cakes and decorations with these nontoxic markers. We use them for drawing fine details and text, and they are easier to control than paintbrushes. The ink is completely edible.

15. **Toothpicks:** Use toothpicks to add food coloring to Royal Icing, fondant, and gum paste, to create stitching details and veins on leaves, and to emboss holes into designs.

16. **Food-coloring gels:** Available in liquid and paste form, these concentrated colorings are used to dye fondant, gum paste, and Royal Icing. To create paint, mix with vodka. Keep in mind that a small quantity yields intense color.

17. **Parchment paper:** We use this oven-safe, nonstick paper as a place for drying fondant and gum-paste decorations, to line cookie sheets and the bottom of cake pans when baking, for rolling out cookie dough (between two sheets), and for tracing designs and creating templates.

NOT PICTURED:

Cornstarch: Dust a clean, flat surface with cornstarch before rolling out fondant to prevent the fondant from sticking.

Glycerin: Add this clear, syrup-like substance to fondant that has dried out and started cracking — just a touch of glycerin can make the dough soft and pliable again. Or brush it on your cake to make fondant look shiny. Glycerin is available online and at cake decorating stores (see Resources, page 217).

Piping gel: This transparent gel serves many decorating purposes. We often use it to attach fondant to nonedible materials such as cake bases or Styrofoam cake dummies. You can tint the gel any color for decorating or writing, or paint it directly on fondant for a shiny finish.

Shortening: Coat your plastic mat with shortening before rolling fondant, gum paste, and marzipan to prevent sticking. Shortening also works for softening hardened gum paste and keeping sugar from sticking to molds. Use a little on your hands when you're rolling any form of sugar dough into balls or ropes.

Baking Terms

We refer often to these sweet substances throughout this book — and as you read our instructions, it can be helpful to know exactly what you're dealing with.

Buttercream: Versatile and sturdy, this classic frosting works beautifully for filling, crumb coating, frosting, and decorating cakes and can be flavored in a variety of delicious ways (page 71).

Crumb coat: When your cake is in its final shape, before you apply the outer layer of rolled fondant or frosting, ice it with a thin layer of frosting to smooth the surface and seal in crumbs. It also helps fondant adhere to the cake (page 40).

Fondant: This is a sweet, pliable dough. At Confetti Cakes we use rolled fondant on most of our projects to create a smooth surface on the outside of cakes. We also use it to make sugar sculptures and decorations (page 80).

Ganache: Made from chopped chocolate and heavy cream, ganache is simple and delicious as a filling or frosting. Because it's so sturdy once it cools, it's a good filling for sculpted cakes (page 77).

Gum paste: This sugar dough is similar in texture to fondant, but it dries quickly and becomes as hard as porcelain. Because of its strength and elasticity, it can be stretched and rolled quite thin and shaped into incredibly detailed decorations. Gum paste's flavor is rather bland, so though it is edible some people prefer to save gum-paste decorations, stored in airtight containers away from heat and humidity, instead of eating them.

Marzipan: Made from almond paste and sugar, this sugar dough has a nice almond taste. Store-bought marzipan generally tastes great and works well for sculpting. You can find it at most grocery stores.

Royal Icing: This is the edible "glue" used to make cake layers adhere to one another. It starts in liquid form but hardens once dry. You can also use it to attach decorations, pipe designs, and ice cookies. The main ingredient is confectioners' sugar, so it's very sweet. It can be dyed any color with food-coloring gels (page 78).

Simple syrup: Add a hint of flavor to cake layers by brushing on a coat of simple syrup, which is made with a combination of boiling water and sugar. Simple syrup keeps cakes and cupcakes moist and can be flavored with the extract or liquor of your choice (page 79).

...

Techniques

....

Τhis section describes the key techniques
you will need to use to make
the cookies, cupcakes, mini cakes, and cakes
in this book. It also includes
tips to help you make a plan for any project,
transport cakes, and deal with
other practical cake decorating matters.

...

Basic Decorating and Cookie Techniques

Dyeing Royal Icing and Buttercream

Start with white Royal Icing or buttercream, and divide it into separate containers for each color you want **before dyeing it.** If you are mixing many colors at once (as for our Lollipop Cookies on page 89), my friend Jeri taught me to use paper cups fitted with lids to store all the colors so they do not dry out. Reserve a little plain white icing in case you make a mistake.

WHAT YOU NEED

Toothpicks

Food-coloring gels

Royal Icing or buttercream

Small offset spatula

METHOD

1. Dip the end of a toothpick into coloring gel so about ¼ inch of it is lightly coated. Dab the color into the icing.

2. Use a small offset spatula to mix the color into the icing until it's thoroughly incorporated and the color is uniform and solid. If you want darker color, repeat the process, adding just a tiny bit of color at a time.

HOT TIPS

* Be **patient** when mixing colors and add color **gradually**. It's time-consuming, but getting the right color is very important for beautiful cakes and cookies.

* It is always easier to add more color than to lighten by adding white icing to a dark color. It's often easier to start with a fresh container of white icing than to try to fix the color.

* Sometimes it is easier to think of colors in temperature. If you want a **warmer** color, add a tiny bit of yellow, and if you want a **cooler** color, add a tiny bit of blue.

Filling a Pastry Bag

WHAT YOU NEED

Scissors

10-inch cloth or plastic pastry bag (we prefer disposable bags for Royal Icing)

Coupler

Pastry tip(s)

Small rubber spatula

Royal Icing (page 78) or other frosting or filling

METHOD

1. Use scissors to cut off the tip of the disposable icing bag.

2. Separate the ring from the bottom of the coupler and insert the bottom piece of the coupler into the pastry bag. It should fit into the tip of the bag. If you are using a large tip, such as #804, you do not need a coupler. Just place the tip directly into the bag.

3. Place the decorating tip onto the coupler and screw the ring over the tip. Make sure there is a tight fit so no icing spills out between the ring and the tip.

4. With the rubber spatula and icing right next to you, form your hand into a C-shape and place the large open end of the pastry bag around the outside of your hand.

5. Use the rubber spatula to fill the bag with icing. Use the C-shape of your hand as a rim to scrape the spatula against as icing falls into the bag. Do not fill the bag more than halfway with stiff icing — you'll have less control when piping.

6. Use the spatula or your hand to push all the icing down toward the tip of the bag. Twist the bag closed and hold it closed as you pipe so icing doesn't squirt out of the back of the bag. When you aren't using a filled bag of icing, keep the open end closed by twisting it back and under the icing on the counter.

HOT TIP

* If the icing is especially runny, place an empty pastry bag fitted with a coupler and pastry tip in the center of a tall glass. Open and fold the back of the pastry bag around the rim of the glass. When the bag is filled, lift it straight out of the glass and use your hands to gather the end of the bag. Push the icing down toward the tip to push out any air bubbles, then twist the bag closed.

Piping

Piping is squeezing small amounts of icing through a narrow pastry tip onto a cake or cookie in a precise pattern. It requires focus and hand-eye coordination and can be difficult to master. The best way to become an expert at it is to practice, practice, practice! Parchment paper is great for practicing piping cookies and specific shapes, and the sides of cake pans are great for trying vertical designs. My friends often tease me for holding my breath while I pipe because it helps my hands stay steady. But that means I have to take breaks so I can breathe and not get a headache!

WHAT YOU NEED

Filled pastry bag

Round pastry tips (use any size to practice; each project in this book suggests which specific tip[s] to use)

METHOD

DOTS

When piping dots, the key is applying the right amount of pressure to the back of the pastry bag. Start applying pressure at a 45-degree angle until you have the size bead you want. Gradually release the pressure **before** you pull the bag away. If you pull back too soon your dots will have peaks. (If you try this many times and still get peaks, you may need looser icing. Add a drop of water at a time until you achieve the desired consistency.) Eventually you will get into a rhythm when piping a series of dots.

STRAIGHT LINES

Begin with your elbows close to your body to keep your hands steady, and hold the pastry bag and tip at a 45-degree angle to your cake or cookie. Touch the icing to the surface and squeeze with constant pressure, then lift the tip away from the surface so the icing can fall while you move your hands toward the intended endpoint of your line. Keep your eyes moving from where you started to where you will finish so you won't be surprised when you reach the end of the line. Try not to drag the tip, because this can clog the point and will not give you a consistent line. To finish the line, gradually stop squeezing and pull up. If you are creating an outline on a cookie, use the outer edge of the cookie as a guide.

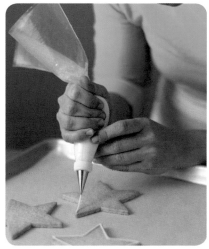

Flooding

Flooding is a method of frosting cookies that creates a smooth, beautiful, glossy finish using Royal Icing. And the sweet icing provides a nice topping to a delicious cookie. To learn how to dye Royal Icing in the hue you need, see page 25.

WHAT YOU NEED

2 pastry bags

Pastry tips: #2, #3

Stiff Royal Icing

Undecorated cookies

Loose Royal Icing

Toothpicks

METHOD

1. Fill a pastry bag fitted with a #2 pastry tip with stiff Royal Icing. Use the shape of the cookie as your guide and pipe a complete outline of the cookie. Make sure there are no gaps in the outline, or the "flood" could spill out. Wait a few minutes to let the outline set before you flood.

2. Use the other pastry bag, fitted with a #3 tip and filled with loose icing, to pipe icing into the center of the cookie. Use a toothpick to drag the icing right up to the piped outline. Do this quickly so the loose icing doesn't set before you've covered the entire surface. The flooded icing should be about ⅛ inch thick.

3. Allow the cookies to dry for about 20 minutes before serving. If you want to add decorations, let them dry for at least 3 hours — and if you are planning to package your cookies to transport or send them, let them dry overnight.

HOT TIPS

* Loose Royal Icing should have the consistency of white glue. To achieve this effect, add water in very small increments to stiff Royal Icing. To check if you have the right consistency, draw a knife through the icing; the mark it makes should disappear after 5 seconds. If it doesn't, add water one drop at a time until you have the consistency you need.

* When you are flooding many cookies, pipe all the outlines first, then do all the flooding.

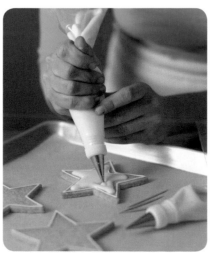

Drop-In Flooding

This method allows you to drop one or more different colors into your flooded background. Have all your colors of flood (looser icing) ready to go in pastry bags before you begin flooding, because you need to do this quickly.

WHAT YOU NEED

Cookies flooded with a pale background color (still wet)

Pastry bags fitted with #2 or #3 pastry tips (the size of the tip determines how much the icing will spread) and filled with the colors of loose Royal Icing you want to add

HOT TIPS

* Run a toothpick directly through the center of a dot that you dropped in to make the shape of a teardrop.

* Avoid dropping dark colors into light backgrounds when using the drop-in flooding technique because dark colors tend to bleed.

METHOD

After you flood the cookie with your background color, squeeze a small amount of the second color directly into the background layer **while it is still wet.** Create polka dots or swirls for a patterned look. See the Lollipop Cookies (page 89) for examples.

Overpiping

Use this technique to create a three-dimensional design or a raised border on flooded cookies that have dried for at least 1 hour.

WHAT YOU NEED

Flooded cookies (dried for at least 1 hour)

Pastry bag fitted with a #1 or #2 tip (or larger if you want a thicker line), filled with stiff Royal Icing

METHOD

Use the same color you used to flood or a contrasting color of icing to pipe design details, monograms, bows, or a raised border on the flooded cookie. Be careful not to drag the pastry tip along the top of the cookie or the line will appear flat. Pipe with the pastry tip hovering slightly above the cookie to create a three-dimensional line.

Decorating with Sanding Sugar

This easy process adds a sparkly layer to cookies.

WHAT YOU NEED

Flooded cookies OR cookies brushed with heated preserves

Sanding sugar

Small bowl

Spoon

METHOD

While the Royal Icing (or preserves) on the cookie is still wet, spoon on a generous layer of sanding sugar, then wait at least 20 minutes for the icing or preserves to dry. Tip the cookies to remove the excess.

HOT TIPS

* Save excess sanding sugar to use again if it isn't attached to any Royal Icing. If you let the icing or preserves dry completely, you'll be able to reuse all your excess.

* Be careful not to fill your cookie with too much icing or the pressure of the sugar could make the flood spill over the outline. If you have used too much icing let the cookie with sanding sugar dry for at least an hour before shaking off the excess sugar. If your cookie does overflow, quickly scrape the entire surface clean of all icing (using a small offset spatula or straight knife) and start again!

Making a Template

Metal cookie cutters make it easy to create a large number of cookies in the exact same shape. If you are making only a few cookies and want to design your own shapes, you can make a cookie template. You can also use this method to cut out templates for cake bases, sugar decorations, and cake.

WHAT YOU NEED

Your desired shape or design

A piece of cardboard or foam core

X-acto knife

Scissors

Rolled-out cookie dough (slightly chilled)

METHOD

Trace or draw your shape on a piece of cardboard or foam core and cut out the shape with an X-acto knife. Trim with scissors if necessary. (If you are using a template from this book, photocopy it and enlarge it to the proper size and then cut.) Place the template on top of the rolled-out cookie dough and use the X-acto knife to cut the shape out of the dough. Transfer the cut-outs to a cookie sheet with an offset spatula, chill, and bake.

HOT TIPS

* For cookies, dip your template (or cutter) in flour before using it to prevent the dough from sticking to it.

* If you are in the habit of making many custom shapes be sure to label them. Once they are filed away it may be difficult to find the shape you are looking for. A binder with plastic sleeves and tabs is a good storage system.

Cupcake Techniques

Creating a Swirl of Frosting

A swirl of frosting is a chic, eye-catching cupcake decoration. Though piping a swirl can seem tricky at first, with a little practice it becomes a simple way to decorate. A cupcake with a swirl on top doesn't need any other adornments, unless you want them, of course! See the Garden Mini Cupcakes on page 115 for an example.

WHAT YOU NEED

Frosting of choice (such as buttercream, ganache, or even chilled lemon curd)

Pastry bag

#12 tip for mini cupcakes or #806 tip for standard size cupcakes.

Baked cupcakes (cooled)

METHOD

1. Spoon the frosting into a pastry bag fitted with a pastry tip of your choice.

2. Start at the outer edge of the cupcake and slowly move the bag in a clockwise motion, piping the icing onto the cupcake. Use the cupcake wrapper as a guide.

3. Each time you pass your starting point, bring the swirl in tighter and higher, and after about 3 times around you should reach the top of the swirl.

HOT TIPS

* Cupcakes look best when the top of the cake hits just below the edge of the wrapper when baked. To achieve this, fill the wrappers just halfway with batter for baking. You may want to test the right batter level with one cupcake before filling and baking them all.

* There are tons of different pastry tips that create all sorts of fun designs besides plain round tips. Have fun and experiment. Star tips make an especially sweet-looking swirl!

Creating a Dome of Filling

If you want to cover a cupcake in fondant — or brown sugar, or chocolate crumbs that resemble "dirt" — it looks best if you begin with a smooth, rounded surface. A dome of filling (such as buttercream or ganache) works perfectly.

WHAT YOU NEED

Baked cupcakes

Filling

Small offset spatula

METHOD

Spoon or pipe a small amount of filling on top of a cupcake. Starting in the center, use a small offset spatula to pull the filling toward the edge of the cupcake, distributing evenly and creating a smooth domed surface about ½ inch thick.

HOT TIP

* If you do not have an offset spatula, a straight knife will also work.

Covering Cupcakes with Fondant

Make cupcakes spectacular and polished looking by covering them with fondant — it's not just for big cakes. See the Counting Cupcakes on page 118 or the Ornament Cupcakes on page 125 for examples.

WHAT YOU NEED

Fondant

Shortening

2½-inch round cutter (for standard size cupcakes)

Baked cupcakes with domes of filling

Fondant smoothers (optional)

Paring knife

METHOD

Roll out fondant to about ⅛ inch thick on a surface coated with shortening. Use the cutter to cut circles of fondant. Place the circles on top of the frosted cupcakes and gently smooth the fondant toward the edges with your hands or fondant smoothers. Cut away any excess fondant with a paring knife.

Cake and Mini Cake Techniques

Splitting Cake

This technique allows you to create layers by slicing through a baked cake horizontally. Setting the cake on a turntable makes this easier, but it's not absolutely necessary.

WHAT YOU NEED

Baked cake

Turntable (optional)

Long serrated knife

Ruler

Cake board

METHOD

1. Set the baked cake on a turntable if you have one. If your cake has risen unevenly, use the long serrated knife to cut off the top rounded surface, creating a flat top surface.

2. Use the ruler to measure the height of the cake so you can divide it evenly. Then use the long serrated knife to cut horizontally through the cake to create two equal layers (or more layers if you baked a higher cake).

3. Transfer the layer that will be the bottom layer onto the cake board, attaching the cake to the board with a dab of buttercream when you are ready to build the cake.

HOT TIPS

* For large cakes, add stability by creating an extra durable cake board. In advance, glue together at least three cardboard pieces, cut to the same size and shape as the bottom cake layer (using an X-acto knife and tracing the shape of the cake pan for exact dimensions), or use a store-bought cake board, before placing the cake on top.

* Once the cake is sculpted you may need to cut away any excess cardboard with scissors or a serrated knife.

Filling Cake

Between the layers of delicious cake you'll want layers of luscious buttercream, ganache, or other filling for the perfect texture and taste.

WHAT YOU NEED

Split cake

Turntable (optional)

Pastry bag fitted with a large round tip (such as #806) OR an offset spatula

Filling of your choice

METHOD

1. Set the split cake on a turntable if you have one. Using a pastry bag fitted with a large round tip, pipe a ½-inch layer of filling over an entire layer of cake. You want layers of filling that are half as thick as the layers of cake — so for 1-inch cake layers, ½ inch of filling is just right. If you don't have a pastry bag and tip, spread on the filling evenly with an offset spatula.

2. Make sure the filling comes out to within ½ inch of the cake edge. Leaving a little room at the edge ensures that the filling will not spill out from the sides when you place the next layer of cake on top.

3. Alternate cake layers with filling layers until you've placed your final layer of cake on top.

HOT TIPS

* When we make a multi-tiered cake, we usually use three layers of cake with two layers of frosting in each tier. Those tiers are approximately 4 inches high.

* If you are brushing your cake with simple syrup, be sure to brush it on the layer **before** adding filling.

Sculpting Cake

Cakes can be much more than round or square shapes! You can create almost any shape you want. First determine the general shape of what you will be carving to help you decide what shape cake to start with. The following are directions for sculpting a **ball** of cake, which you'll need for the Monster Cake (page 193); this shape is great to learn for sports balls, domes, and so many other cakes you might dream up.

WHAT YOU NEED

Round or square block of split and filled cake, about the height you want your ball to be

Turntable (optional)

Small serrated knives

METHOD

1. Set the cake on a turntable if you have one. Use a serrated knife to trim the edges off your block of cake and to cut the cake to the approximate width you want your ball to be at its widest point.

2. Using a smaller serrated knife, carve away small pieces of cake at a time to create a ball shape. Remember, go slowly. It's like a haircut — once you cut it off it's too late to glue it back on!

3. When the ball shape is complete, trim away the excess cake board to fit the new shape — and you're ready to crumb coat.

HOT TIPS

* Although cake pans come in many shapes we find them unreliable because of shrinking and uneven baking. If you bake half-sheets of cake instead, your cake will bake evenly and you can cut whatever shape layers you desire from the rectangle.

* When carving cakes into specific shapes, you might want to start with a larger block of split and filled cake than you think you need — then carve away just a little at a time.

* There are pans that come in two half-spheres to help you make a ball shape, but they do not give you the flexibility to determine your own size, and the two halves are stuck together with just one layer of filling, unless you split the cakes.

Crumb Coating

This technique makes the outside of your cake smooth and prepares it to be covered in fondant.

WHAT YOU NEED

Small serrated knife

Split and filled (and sculpted, if you are sculpting) cake

Offset spatula

Filling

METHOD

1. Use a small serrated knife to trim any protruding edges from the cake that are not part of your intended shape, if necessary. To create a perfectly smooth fondant-covered cake, you need a uniform crumb coat.

2. Use an offset spatula to smooth any extra filling oozing out from between layers. Add a little more filling and spread it into a thin layer all over the outside of your cake. Be sure to create an even surface. If you have time, let the cake sit for several hours or overnight in the refrigerator so it can chill and settle before you cover it with fondant.

Covering Cake with Fondant

Once your cake is crumb coated and the cake board is trimmed to fit, it's ready to be covered with fondant. I always think of this as the second phase of cake design. Before you begin working with fondant, make sure your work space is clear of extra cake, crumbs, and clutter. Place your cake in the refrigerator after you've crumb coated, while you are rolling out the fondant. Chill the cake for 10 to 20 minutes just before you cover — it helps to firm up the final shape.

Described here is the method for covering round cakes; instructions for covering square cakes and irregularly shaped cakes (such as the ball cake) and for piecing fondant follow on page 44. Round cakes are generally the easiest to cover because the fondant drapes easily over the edges. However, covering cakes that are otherwise shaped is not much different, so don't be afraid to try. It just takes practice!

WHAT YOU NEED

Small strainer

Cornstarch

Fondant in the amount and colors your project requires

Rolling pin

Ruler

Fondant smoothers

Dry pastry brush

Split, filled, and crumb-coated cake

Paring knife

METHOD

1. Using a small strainer, dust a flat, clean surface with cornstarch to prevent the fondant from sticking.

2. Unwrap the fondant and knead it until it becomes soft, then shape it into a round ball and flatten slightly.

3. Use a rolling pin to roll out the fondant — just like you'd roll out cookie dough. As you get started, turn the fondant a few times to make sure it's even on all sides and that it is not sticking to your surface. Roll it out so the surface area is larger than the cake you need to cover and is about ¼ inch thick. As you are rolling it out, keep in mind that you need to cover the sides of the cake as well as the top surface.

4. While the fondant is still rolled out on the flat surface, run the fondant smoothers over it to even it out.

5. Pick up the fondant by rolling it gently onto a rolling pin, wiping off any excess cornstarch with a dry pastry brush as you go. Once all the fondant is around the rolling pin, carefully unroll it over the cake.

6. Starting on top of the cake, smooth the surface of the fondant with your hands. Continue along the sides of the cake, gently pressing the fondant to the cake. Do not press the fondant onto itself — it will wrinkle. After the cake is completely covered, gently pull the fondant away from the cake, then smooth it back down, like smoothing the pleats of a skirt. Run the fondant smoothers all over the cake to create a completely smooth surface.

7. When the cake is entirely covered, cut away any excess fondant with a paring knife. First cut away the bulk of the excess, leaving a 1-inch border. Then use the side of your hand to create a crease where the fondant meets the side of the cake and the table. Make a final cut around the bottom of the cake, leaving a straight edge.

HOT TIP

* If possible, allow the fondant-covered cake to sit overnight before you decorate it to give it a chance to settle and to make handling it easier.

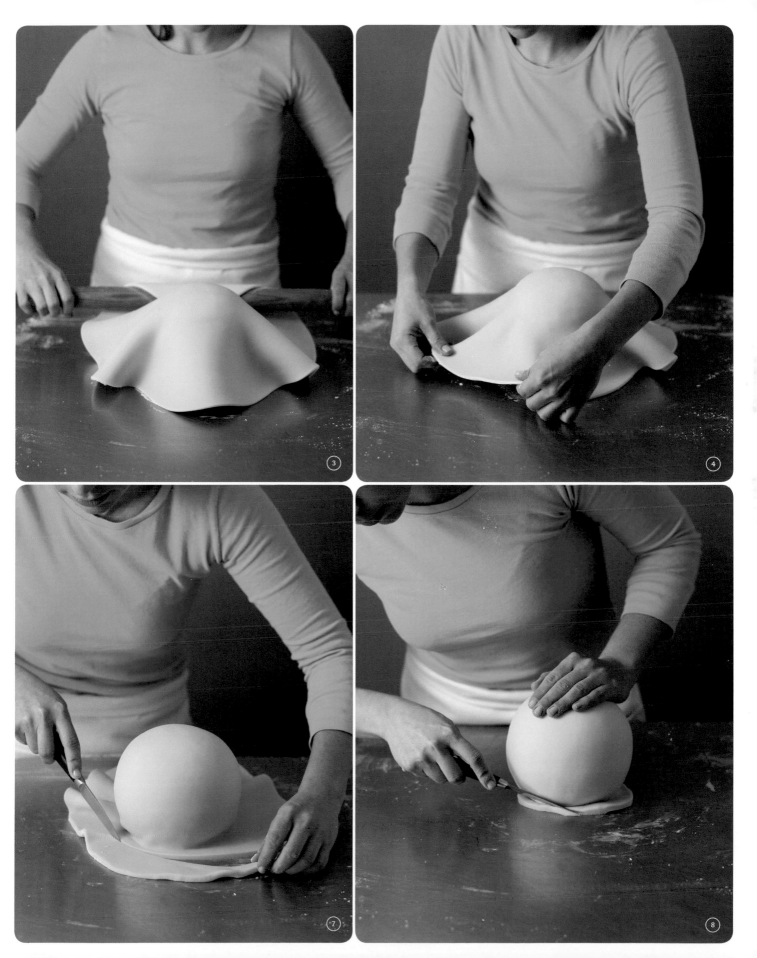

Square Cakes

Use the basic method for covering cakes in fondant, paying close attention to the corners. If the fondant it too dry or heavy, the corners of your cake might begin to crack or the edges could become weighted down. To keep this from happening, make sure your fondant is rolled out to ¼ inch (no thicker) and moist enough. You'll know it's too dry if it is cracking before you roll it out. To moisten fondant, knead some shortening or glycerin into it and try to work quickly.

As soon as you cover the cake, use your hands and fondant smoothers to press the fondant into the sides of the cake and manipulate it carefully around the corners.

Sculpted and Irregularly Shaped Cakes

For cakes in fun shapes like a ball, you can still cover the cake all at once, with one piece of fondant. Work carefully around any irregular parts and if there are any corners, pay extra attention to those areas and press the fondant carefully against the cake. However, if your cake is too wide or too tall for that, you can try piecing fondant together.

Piecing Fondant

This technique allows you to cover a cake of any size and shape in fondant. It makes covering large cakes much easier. It's also good for cakes that have an open space on top where they are filled with something other than fondant, such as the Beach Pail Cupcakes on page 129. When piecing fondant, try to place seams in logical spots (such as along the seams or edges in the Backpack Cake on page 201) so the piecing will be less obvious.

METHOD

1. Start by rolling out the fondant to ¼ inch thick on a cutting board covered with shortening (to prevent sticking).

2. Use a paring knife and a ruler (or a template, if using) to cut out pieces into the appropriate sizes for the sections of cake you need to cover.

3. Slide an offset spatula under the pieces of fondant to release them from the cutting board. Gently apply them to the cake. If the fondant does not stick well, brush the back of it with a little water to make it stick better.

Covering a Cake Base with Fondant

This technique makes a large cake base look like it belongs with your cake. You should do this a couple days ahead of time so it can dry completely. Use a store-bought foil cake drum or make your own base using cardboard or foam core. Wrap the base in tin foil and secure it with tape, making sure it can lie completely flat on a table. Roll enough fondant to cover your cake board to ¼ inch thick (we specify amounts in each recipe). Brush your cake board with water or piping gel and cover it with the fondant, smoothing and cutting the edges as if you were covering a cake. Set it aside to dry for at least 24 hours, and preferably for 2 days, before you place cake on it.

Making a Structurally Sound Cake

* Structural security is the most important internal element of your cake (other than how it tastes, of course). There are many factors to take into consideration.

* Always store your cake at the proper temperature. Cool or cold is better than hot. Fondant-covered cakes should be stored in a cool or air-conditioned room (but not refrigerated, because the humidity could cause it to sweat when you remove it from the fridge).

* Pay attention to the density of your cakes. They shouldn't be dry or heavy, but they shouldn't be delicate or super crumbly, either.

* For cakes over 4 inches high, we always use dowels. Adding that structural support keeps cakes intact and protects all your hard work.

Doweling Tiered Cakes

Our cakes with multiple tiers don't miraculously defy gravity — they have good internal support from dowels. Do **not** use plastic drinking straws as dowels; they can collapse easily and they can slide around in moist cake, which threatens the integrity of your cake's structure.

The best dowels to use are plastic tubes, which are strong enough to handle even the heaviest of cakes. They are available in cake decorating stores (see Resources, page 217) and some hardware stores. Wooden dowels also work, and they are especially great for small cakes with narrow areas, or for running down the center of a tall cake. You can find them at hardware stores. You'll need to cut your dowels to the exact height of the tiers into which you plan to insert them. (See photo on page 46.)

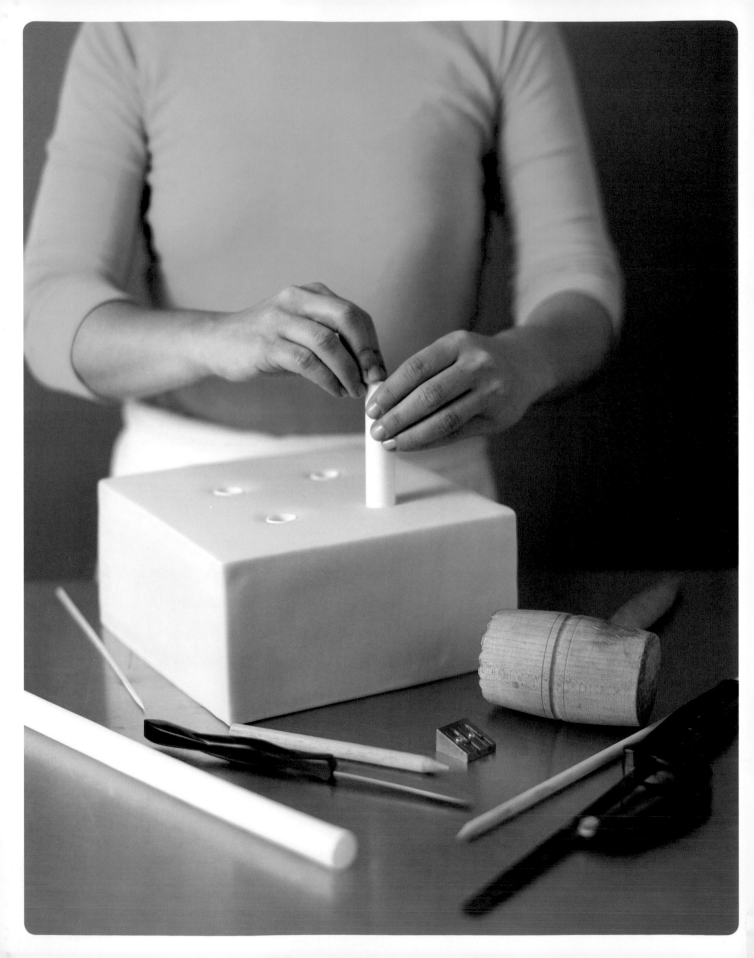

Doweling Sculpted Cakes

If you are making a sculpted cake taller than 4 inches, you need to dowel it for support **before** adding the layers above 4 inches. This will all take place before you crumb coat and cover with fondant. You will be doweling **inside** the cake. Insert dowels directly into the bottom 4 inches. Then place a piece of foam core, cut into the shape of the cake but an inch smaller on all sides, beneath the next layers.

WHAT YOU NEED

Finished cake tiers on cake boards

Royal Icing

White glue (only if attaching cake to a base)

Wooden skewers

Pen

Serrated knife (or hand saw)

Plastic or wooden dowels

Palette knife

Fondant smoothers (optional)

Pencil sharpener (only if doweling an entire tall cake)

Mallet or hammer (only if doweling an entire tall cake)

METHOD

1. Glue the bottom tier of cake (each tier is on its own cake board) onto your cake base using Royal Icing or nontoxic white glue. (No one will be eating the cardboard.)

2. Insert a wooden skewer into the center of the tier. Use a pen to mark where the top of the cake hits the skewer. Pull the skewer out and use it as a guide to cut the dowels to the proper size with a serrated knife or small handsaw. The number of dowels you'll use depends on the size of your cake and the size of the next tier.

3. For an average size cake (9 inches), place one dowel in the center of the tier and five or six dowels in a ring around the center. If the tier is much wider than the first ring, create another ring, being careful to stay within the confines of the next tier. You don't want to be able to see the dowels when the next tier is in place. To avoid confusion, use a cardboard round or the bottom of a cake pan that's the size of the next tier to create an imaginary border.

4. Once the dowels are inserted straight into the cake, spread Royal Icing all over the doweled area, again staying within the confines of the next tier.

5. Using a palette knife, carefully place the next tier on top of the doweled tier and center it. Use your hands or fondant smoothers to adjust the position of the cake. The Royal Icing doesn't dry immediately so you have a few minutes to work with, but after that the tier should stay where it is.

6. If your cake involves more than two tiers, repeat steps 2, 3, and 4. Don't dowel the top tier unless you plan to top it with a heavy decoration.

7. If your cake is more than two tiers high, I suggest placing one long dowel through the entire cake, from top to bottom. This is a very good idea if you will be transporting the cake; it will keep the tiers from shifting. Measure the height of the entire cake, not including the cake base. Cut the dowel to the right length and use a pencil sharpener to sharpen one end of the dowel. Guide the sharpened point straight into the center of the top tier. When you feel it hit the cardboard, use a wooden mallet or hammer (gently but firmly) to guide the dowel straight down through the whole cake.

HOT TIPS

* We often use a combination of wooden and plastic dowels. Wooden dowels are thinner and work better for smaller tiers; plastic dowels are wider and take up more room.

* Make sure each tier, or every 4 inches of cake, has a cake board underneath it for support.

Deconstructing Cakes

After all the time you spend building your cakes, you need to take them apart so people can enjoy eating them.

For cakes made out of distinct tiers, slide a cake server (or any other flat metal spatula) under the cardboard of each tier and remove it before cutting. Start at the top and lift off each tier as you work your way down. If a cake is made out of multiple layers within the overall shape of the cake (such as the Monster Cake on page 193) and you can't tell where the dowels are, cut straight down until you hit cardboard. Serve slices from that tier of cake, remove the cake board and dowels, and begin cutting the next tier.

For cakes that involve multiple pieces of cake and many sugar decorations, it's easiest to deconstruct the entire cake before serving it. Start by removing any sugar decorations attached with wire and separate the individual pieces of cake. For example, to deconstruct the Gift Box Cake (page 159), remove the bow from the lid then separate the lid from the box and remove all the tissue paper before cutting it into pieces to serve.

HOT TIP

* Remove the dowels before serving. If you make the cake as a gift be sure to explain to the host where the dowels are located.

Decorating Techniques for Fondant, Gum Paste, and Marzipan

Deciding Whether to Use Fondant, Gum Paste, or Marzipan

Fondant is sweet, soft, and quite malleable and it stiffens slightly on the outside but stays soft inside after it has set. It is best used for covering entire cakes or for decorations that don't need much support. Marzipan is similar in consistency to fondant and has a delicious almond flavor, but should not be used for decorations that need total stability, such as the tiara on page 173 or the loop bows on page 55. Gum paste can be rolled very thin, but because it contains an edible element called gum tragacanth, it dries very hard. Gum paste is best for detailed decorations or decorations that need to stand on their own structurally. These three different doughs are not interchangeable, so it's a good idea to use the ones we suggest in the instructions for the projects in this book.

Storing Fondant, Gum Paste, and Marzipan

Fondant, gum paste, and marzipan can dry out quickly. Even if you are taking just a short break, keep them tightly wrapped in plastic wrap. When you are finished with them for the day, double wrap them in plastic wrap and seal them in an airtight container. Never get them wet because they'll become too sticky to handle. Store them at room temperature. Do not store cakes decorated with any three of these doughs in the refrigerator, because the humidity could make the cake sweat and the decorations wither once they come out. Store the cake uncovered in the coolest (and safest!) spot in your house.

HOT TIPS

* If your rolled out gum paste is getting dry too quickly, cover it with a piece of plastic wrap and place a damp cloth on top of the plastic, never letting the damp cloth touch the gum paste.

* If you are making many gum paste decorations that you want to dry quickly and you live in a hot and humid climate, use a dehumidifier.

Dyeing Fondant, Gum Paste, and Marzipan

Create surfaces and decorations in any color you want by dyeing white fondant, gum paste, and marzipan (all sugar doughs) with food coloring.

WHAT YOU NEED

White fondant, gum paste, or marzipan

Toothpick

Gel or liquid food coloring

METHOD

1. Place the sugar dough on a clean surface. Use a toothpick to add a tiny bit of food coloring directly to the dough. Remember that food coloring is extremely concentrated, so you do not need to add much to get a lot of color. Err on the side of using less than you need, because you can always add more.

2. Knead the fondant, gum paste, or marzipan with the coloring until it's completely incorporated. For a marble look, twist the color so the stripes are evenly distributed throughout the dough and roll it out. If you want a solid color, knead until the color is completely mixed throughout the dough.

Painting with Powders and Dusts

To paint using food-coloring powders, luster dusts, and petal dusts, create a mixture of small amounts of the power or dust and lemon extract to form a liquid pigment. For every ¼ teaspoon of powder or dust, start with a drop or two of extract. Add enough extract to form a smooth liquid paint, but not too much or the mixture will be thin and will not coat the surface evenly. Paint onto a smooth surface with a paintbrush. We use this technique for several projects in this book, including the Ornament Cupcakes (page 125) and the MP3 Mini Cakes (page 151).

Painting with Food-Coloring Gels

Mix small amounts of food-coloring gels with a few drops of vodka to create a paint mixture. The more coloring you use, the darker the pigment will be. To lighten the color, add more vodka.

WOOD STAINING

This technique makes fondant look just like a wooden surface — a delicious, edible wooden surface! The amount of materials you'll need depends on whether you're making something small like buttons or something large like a cake base. We use this technique for the Toy Train Cake (page 177) and the Sock Monkey Cake (page 185).

WHAT YOU NEED

White fondant

Brown food-coloring gel

Rolling pin

Vodka

Paintbrush with stiff bristles

METHOD

1. Divide the fondant in half and dye one portion light brown.

2. Roll the 2 pieces of fondant into long skinny ropes, one white and one light brown.

3. Twist the fondant ropes together so the brown becomes marbled into the white. Don't twist too much — you want to leave some of the white fondant showing.

4. Roll out the fondant and place it on a cake or cake base.

5. Mix 2 tablespoons of vodka and a small drop of brown food coloring in a small dish. Use this as paint, and with a paintbrush, apply a thin coat to the surface of your "wood."

6. Add more food coloring to the vodka mixture to make it darker, and paint small irregular marks like you would see in real wood. Using a brush with stiff bristles will help create the thin lines found in a real piece of wood.

HOT TIPS

* Use an actual piece of wood or a photograph of real wood as a model while you are painting to help you create a realistic pattern.

* For a rustic look, use a paring knife to make rough markings all over the surface of the fondant before you paint.

* Cut long lines in a base with a paring knife to create the look of the individual slats of a wooden floor, then make holes with a toothpick at either end of the slats to show nail holes.

Using a Pasta Machine

Pasta machines aren't just for pasta! Cake decorators use them to create very thin sheets of gum paste or fondant for decorations. They save a lot of time and energy and render a consistent thickness throughout. In this book we use them to roll out gum paste for stripes and to make loop bows (page 55).

WHAT YOU NEED

Pasta machine

Rolling pin

Gum paste or fondant

METHOD

1. Attach the pasta machine to a flat surface and make sure the crank is on the outside so you can turn it. You should also make sure there is enough space for the sugar dough to come through onto the surface.

2. Using the rolling pin, form a flattened square of gum paste or fondant into a sheet thin enough (about $\frac{1}{16}$ inch) to squeeze through the largest opening of the pasta machine.

3. Feed the rolled-out gum paste or fondant into the top opening of the machine and turn the crank to roll it through the machine.

4. Run the gum paste or fondant through the machine as many times as you need to, using a smaller setting each time, until you achieve your desired thickness.

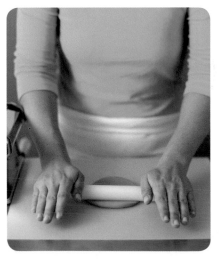 

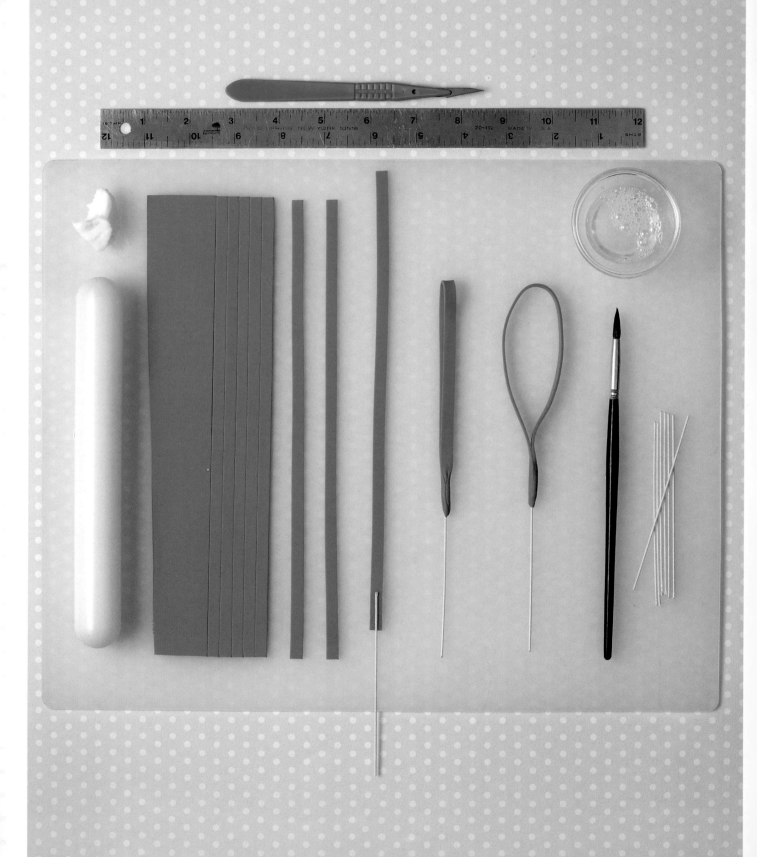

Making Loop Bows

A cake adorned with a festive loop bow made from dozens of delicate individual loops makes any occasion a celebration. Below we describe the method that you should use for the Gift Box Cake (page 159). You could also decorate the Quinceañera Cake (page 171) with loop bows instead of a tiara.

WHAT YOU NEED

Parchment paper

Gum paste

Plastic mat, shortening, and rolling pin or pasta machine

Ruler

Scalpel or paring knife

Small paintbrush

Egg whites

Cloth-covered wires

METHOD

1. Cover a flat surface — or several cookie sheets or trays so you can move them — with parchment paper. This is where you will let the individual loops rest before assembly.

2. Roll gum paste (about 6 ounces for the Gift Box Cake) into a sheet approximately 1/16 inch thick (either on a plastic mat greased with shortening using a rolling pin, or through a pasta machine). Cut the gum paste into strips 1/4 inch wide and 10 inches long using a scalpel or paring knife. (You will need to re-roll the gum paste to get enough strips.)

You need about 55 loops to create the large bow of the Gift Box Cake, and you should make a few extra in case of breakage.

3. Dip a brush in the egg whites and coat the lower third of each strip on one side. Place a cloth-covered wire so it extends about 1 inch into the gum paste strip, over the egg white–brushed portion.

4. Fold over the top of the strip and pinch the wire between the two ends of gum paste to seal it. Shape the strip into a loop and set it on its side on parchment paper to dry for at least 1 week.

Using Egg Whites or Water as "Glue"

Cake designers most often use Royal Icing as an edible glue to attach decorations to cakes, but sometimes when you want decorations to lie completely flat on the surface of a cake or cookie and do not want the icing to show, liquid works better. Egg whites have a natural binding composition and are especially great for attaching parts of a sugar sculpture together. Egg whites purchased in their own container from a store are the best because they are usually ultra-pasteurized.

Either water or egg whites applied with a paintbrush will do the trick. Generally we prefer to use egg whites because, once dry, they have a stronger hold. But if you know someone is allergic or you do not have egg whites on hand, water is fine.

A third option for liquid glue is Royal Icing thinned to liquid consistency with either water or egg whites. This color will be opaque, not clear, but the bind will be very strong. It will take a little longer to dry than stiff Royal Icing. Whatever you choose, use only a small amount, because both the water and the egg whites will appear shiny when dry.

Practical Techniques

Making a Plan

Without a doubt, the most important step in the process of cake decoration is making a plan. Start with a photograph or a sketch of the project you wish to complete, and think about what needs to be done first. Be sure to take all of the following elements into account.

SERVINGS: Determine the number of people the cake needs to serve. The size of the cake has an impact on everything from your cake base to the number of sugar decorations needed to the size of the box it will fit in if you plan to transport it. We tell you how many servings all the projects in this book provide. But if you are changing the project or doing something on your own, for a tiered cake you calculate the number of servings by adding together the number of servings in each tier (refer to the servings chart on page 70). For sculpted cakes, bake more cake than you think you need to allow extra cake for carving. Remember, even if you bake the most adorable cake, if there isn't enough to eat, you (and everyone who wants some) will be sorry!

BASES: Having the right base is key for decorating and transporting. For heavier cakes, we suggest using a wood base, wrapped in foil and then covered so it looks pretty, of course. For smaller cakes you can use cake bases that come already covered in foil (available at cake decorating stores) or make your own base from layers of cardboard or foam core glued together. At Confetti Cakes, we cover all our cake bases in fondant for a clean look that coordinates with the rest of the cake. If you can, cover your cake base at least one day in advance so it has time to set.

SUGAR DECORATIONS: Decorations made from gum paste or fondant usually need a few days to dry before you can use them safely. Determine how much time you need, make the decorations ahead, and set them aside in a place where they won't be knocked over!

BAKING: When baking cakes, keep your final design plan and sculpting needs in mind. Bake in round pans for cylindrical cakes and square pans for more geometric cakes. For an irregular design, baking in half-sheet pans is usually best, as this allows you to create whatever shape you need.

FILLINGS: Make fillings and frostings while your cakes are cooling. You can use one flavor for the whole cake, or use different flavors in the different tiers of cake.

HOT TIP

* When making cakes for kids, remember that though their eyes get very big when they see the cake, their tummies are small, and they probably only need a serving about half the size of an adult serving.

Transporting Cookies, Cupcakes, and Cakes

One of the questions we are always asked is, "How did you get that here?!?" After all the time you spend on your cakes, you don't want to damage them when you move them. Bakery boxes are fine for lightweight items, but generally we prefer to use heavy-duty, corrugated boxes. No matter what kind of box you use, make sure it stays level.

COOKIES: Make sure cookies are completely dry before you bag or box them. Separate layers with pieces of parchment paper.

CUPCAKES: Refrigerate cupcakes decorated with ganache or buttercream before boxing them. If they are covered with fondant they can sit out overnight, but box them as soon as they are ready to go. The bottom of the box should be totally flat and very sturdy. Line up one row, then arrange the next row, with each cupcake set between two cupcakes in the first row to keep them from shifting in the box.

CAKES: Use a corrugated cardboard box 2 inches wider than your cake base — when you center the cake base in the box, there should be 1 inch of extra room on each side, enough so the cake doesn't touch the box, but not too much. If your cake is more than four tiers high, or if it features fragile or heavy sugar decorations, don't assemble the cake until you arrive at the location where it will be served. In addition, be sure to:

1. Reinforce the bottom of the box with packing tape — many times!

2. Cut open one side of the box so you can slide the cake in and keep it level.

3. Put some packing tape in the middle of the box, creating a loop out of the tape so it will stick to the bottom of the box and the bottom of your cake base, before placing the cake. This will prevent the cake from sliding around. Tape the box closed.

4. If you're driving, place the cake in your car with protection on all sides to keep the box from shifting, and if it's hot, crank up the air conditioning before you place the cake in the car.

5. Before you remove the cake from the car, find out exactly where it will be going. When you get it there, carefully cut all the sides of the box open and use an offset spatula to lift the cake out of the box, removing the tape from the bottom of the base.

...

Basic Recipes

. . . .

Everything we make at Confetti Cakes tastes
as incredible as it looks.
And that's especially important when we're
making cakes for kids. They love to look at the fun,
amazing, delightful creations—
and they can't wait to eat them. The recipes here are
our favorites for cakes, cookies,
brownies, fillings, and icings that work beautifully
with the projects in this book, and that have delighted
hundreds of our toughest customers: kids!

...

One thing that makes our cakes and cookies taste so good is that we use the very best ingredients. Doing the same thing at home will help you achieve excellent results. Look for the very best cocoa powder and chocolate—we like Valrhona cocoa powder and Scharffen Berger chocolate bars — and use pure extracts (not imitation) if possible. Also use unsalted butter and whole milk when baking — otherwise the flavor and texture may be off.

Having the right ingredients is a good place to start. Then, before you dive into beating and stirring, be sure to read through the entire recipe so you know exactly what you'll need to do and there are no surprises. With baking, you should always measure precisely and follow instructions closely. Sift the flour and the cocoa, and chop the chocolate as directed. Try not to skip steps. The results just won't be the same. If you give yourself plenty of time and follow the recipes closely, baking in your kitchen will be rewarding and fun — and the final product will be delicious! Note: for all the recipes that require baking, we give the temperature in Fahrenheit (°F). To convert to Celsius, subtract 32 from the Fahrenheit number, divide by 9, and multiply by 5.

Vanilla Sugar Cookies

YIELD: approximately twelve 3-inch cookies

My grandmomi Pearl used to make these cookies for me, and they have been my favorites since I was a little girl. Buttery and scented with vanilla, they are great for cutting into shapes and decorating. For the best shape, it's important to freeze the cut cookies for at least 15 minutes or until they are firm to the touch (this helps prevent spreading) before you bake them.

WHAT YOU NEED

2⅓ cups plus 2 tablespoons (11 ounces) all-purpose flour

1 teaspoon salt

1 teaspoon baking powder

¾ cup (6 ounces; 1½ sticks) unsalted butter

½ cup plus 2 tablespoons (4 ounces) granulated sugar

1 large egg

1 teaspoon pure vanilla extract

METHOD

1. In a medium bowl, sift together the flour, salt, and baking powder. Set aside.

2. In the bowl of a standing mixer fitted with a paddle attachment, combine the butter and sugar and beat on medium speed until light and fluffy. Add the egg and vanilla and beat until combined.

3. Add the flour mixture in 2 batches, scraping down the bowl after each addition. Beat until the dough just comes together, being careful not to overmix.

4. Turn out the dough onto a lightly floured surface. Form the dough into a ball, wrap it in plastic, and refrigerate for 30 minutes.

5. Place the ball of dough between two pieces of parchment paper and roll out to ¼ inch thick. Keeping the dough in the parchment, transfer to a cookie sheet and place in the refrigerator for at least 1 hour.

6. Cut the cookies in the desired shapes and place at least 1 inch apart on a half-sheet pan lined with parchment paper or an ungreased nonstick cookie sheet. Transfer to the freezer and chill for at least 15 minutes or until they are stiff.

7. Preheat the oven to 350°F.

8. Bake until the cookies are light golden brown, about 10 minutes.

9. Let the cookies cool completely on the sheets before decorating. (They will still be soft when they come out of the oven and may break or become misshapen if they are moved off the sheets before cool.)

VARIATIONS

CITRUS COOKIES: Add 1 teaspoon of finely grated lemon or orange zest to the butter and sugar mixture in step 2.

ALMOND COOKIES: Replace the vanilla with 1 teaspoon pure almond extract.

HOT TIP

* You can make this dough up to 2 weeks ahead of time. Roll out the dough between two pieces of parchment paper, wrap in plastic, and freeze. Defrost until the dough is pliable enough to roll out to the desired thickness and cut, 10 to 15 minutes. Continue from step 6.

Chocolate Cookies

YIELD: approximately twelve 3-inch cookies

Use the best quality bittersweet chocolate you can find (or semisweet if that's all you have) for these crisp, addictive chocolate cookies. The dough is ideal for rolling out and cutting into fun, whimsical shapes.

WHAT YOU NEED

- 2⅓ cups plus 2 tablespoons (11 ounces) all-purpose flour
- ¼ teaspoon salt
- ½ teaspoon baking soda
- 6 ounces bittersweet chocolate, chopped or morsels
- 1 cup (8 ounces; 2 sticks) unsalted butter
- 1½ cups (8 ounces) granulated sugar
- 1 large egg
- 1 teaspoon pure vanilla extract

METHOD

1. In a medium bowl, sift together the flour, salt, and baking soda. Set aside.

2. Place the chocolate in a double boiler and melt over medium heat. Alternatively, place the chocolate in a bowl and microwave in 15-second increments, stirring between increments. Be careful not to let the chocolate burn.

3. In the bowl of a standing mixer fitted with a paddle attachment, combine the butter and sugar and beat on medium speed until light and fluffy. Add the egg and vanilla and beat until combined.

4. Set the mixer to low speed and add the melted chocolate.

5. Add the flour mixture in 2 batches, scraping down the bowl after each addition. Beat until the dough just comes together, being careful not to overmix.

6. Turn out the dough onto a lightly floured surface. Form the dough into a ball, wrap it in plastic, and refrigerate for 30 minutes.

7. Place the dough between two pieces of parchment paper and roll out to ¼ inch thick. Transfer the dough to the refrigerator and chill for at least 1 hour.

8. Cut out cookies in the desired shapes and place at least 1 inch apart on a half-sheet pan lined with parchment paper or an ungreased nonstick cookies sheet. Transfer to the refrigerator and chill for at least 15 minutes or until they are stiff.

9. Preheat the oven to 350°F.

10. Bake until the cookies are firm to the touch, about 10 minutes.

11. Let the cookies cool completely before decorating.

HOT TIP

* You can make this dough up to 2 weeks ahead of time. Roll out the dough between two pieces of parchment paper, wrap in plastic, and freeze. Defrost until the dough is pliable enough to roll out to the desired thickness and cut, 10 to 15 minutes. Continue from step 8.

Gingerbread Cookies

YIELD: approximately twelve 3-inch cookies

Ginger and spices add a flavorful kick to these fragrant cookies, which are the best holiday treats, especially if you cut them into adorable gingerbread girl and boy shapes (see page 96 for decorating ideas).

WHAT YOU NEED

3¾ cups (16 ounces) all-purpose flour

¾ teaspoon salt

¾ teaspoon baking soda

1 tablespoon ground ginger

1 tablespoon ground cinnamon

¾ teaspoon ground cloves

¾ teaspoon ground nutmeg

¾ cup (6 ounces; 1½ sticks) unsalted butter

1 cup plus 2 tablespoons (8 ounces) packed, dark brown sugar

3 egg yolks

2 tablespoons molasses

METHOD

1. In a medium bowl, sift together the flour, salt, baking soda, ginger, cinnamon, cloves, and nutmeg. Set aside.

2. In the bowl of a standing mixer fitted with a paddle attachment, combine the butter and brown sugar and beat on medium speed until light and fluffy.

3. Set the mixer to low speed and gradually add the egg yolks and molasses, scraping often, and beat until combined.

4. Add the flour mixture in 2 batches, scraping down the bowl after each addition. Beat until the dough just comes together, being careful not to overmix.

5. Turn out the dough onto a lightly floured surface. Form the dough into a ball, wrap it in plastic, and refrigerate for 30 minutes.

6. Place the ball of dough between two pieces of parchment paper and roll out to ¼ inch thick. Keeping the dough in the parchment, transfer to a cookie sheet and place in the refrigerator for at least 1 hour.

7. Cut the cookies in the desired shapes and place on a half-sheet pan lined with parchment paper or an ungreased nonstick cookie sheet, at least 1 inch apart. Transfer to the freezer and chill for at least 15 minutes or until they are stiff.

8. Preheat the oven to 350°F.

9. Bake until the cookies are firm to the touch and are slightly browned on the edges, about 10 minutes.

10. Let cookies cool completely before decorating.

HOT TIP

* You can make this dough up to 2 weeks ahead of time. Roll out the dough between two pieces of parchment paper, wrap in plastic, and freeze. Defrost until the dough is pliable enough to roll out to the desired thickness and cut, 10 to 15 minutes. Continue from step 7.

Amazing Chocolate Brownies

YIELD: 1 half-sheet (13 x 18 inches), approximately forty 2-inch squares

I learned how to make these rich, decadent brownies when I was in pastry school, and I've never found a brownie recipe that I like better. They are dense and more like fudge than cake. Use them to make our Slice of Cake Brownie Mini Cakes (page 135) — or snack on them anytime you or your kids have a serious chocolate craving.

WHAT YOU NEED

2 cups (8 ounces) all-purpose flour

2 cups (16 ounces; 4 sticks) unsalted butter

16 ounces bittersweet chocolate

8 eggs

½ teaspoon salt

2¼ cups (16 ounces) granulated sugar

2¼ cups (16 ounces) packed dark brown sugar

1 tablespoon pure vanilla extract

METHOD

1. Preheat the oven to 350°F. Brush the bottom and sides of a half-sheet pan with melted butter and line the bottom with parchment paper.

2. Sift the flour into a large bowl. Set aside.

3. In a double boiler, melt the butter and chocolate together over low heat.

4. In the bowl of a standing mixer fitted with a paddle attachment, combine the eggs, salt, granulated sugar, brown sugar, and vanilla and beat on low speed until combined.

5. Slowly add the chocolate mixture and beat on low speed until combined.

6. Remove the bowl from the mixer and gently fold in the flour, using a rubber spatula.

7. Pour the batter into the prepared pan. Bake for about 1 hour, or until the top has formed a shiny crust and is moderately firm.

8. Allow the brownies to cool for 20 minutes before removing them from the pan. When cool, release the brownies from the pan by running a metal spatula or knife along the sides of the pan. Flip the brownies over onto another pan or cake board and peel away the parchment.

HOT TIPS

* Brownies can be stored in the freezer for up to 2 weeks, tightly wrapped in at least two layers of plastic wrap.

* For easier cutting, freeze the brownies overnight, then remove from the freezer, and allow to defrost slightly (about 30 minutes), then cut with a chef's knife.

Chocolate Cake

YIELD: three 9-inch rounds, 1 half-sheet (13 x 18 inches), or 24 cupcakes

This is the best chocolate cake I've ever tasted. It's the same chocolate cake we feature in *The Confetti Cakes Cookbook*, because it's our most requested, most decadent cake. Kids of all ages adore it. Use the highest quality cocoa you can find, and you will taste the difference. Good quality cocoa will be dark chocolate brown and have an intense chocolaty smell. I love pairing this with Vanilla Buttercream (page 71). The cake is so rich, and a light, not-too-sweet filling is perfect with it.

WHAT YOU NEED

2⅔ cups (12 ounces) all-purpose flour

1¼ cups plus 2 tablespoons (4 ounces) unsweetened cocoa powder

2 teaspoons baking powder

1 teaspoon baking soda

1 teaspoon salt

1 cup (8 ounces) sour cream

1 teaspoon pure vanilla extract

1 teaspoon pure almond extract

1 cup (2 sticks; 8 ounces) unsalted butter

2 cups (14 ounces) granulated sugar

2 eggs

1¼ cups (10 ounces) strong prepared nonflavored coffee

METHOD

1. Preheat the oven to 350°F. Brush the bottoms and sides of the pans with melted butter and line the bottoms with parchment paper.

2. In a large bowl, sift together the all-purpose flour, cocoa powder, baking powder, baking soda, and salt. Set aside.

3. In a separate bowl, combine the sour cream, vanilla, and almond extract. Set aside.

4. In the bowl of a standing mixer fitted with a paddle attachment, combine the butter and sugar and beat on medium speed until smooth.

5. Set the mixer to low speed and add the eggs, one at a time, scraping thoroughly between additions.

6. Alternately add the flour and sour cream mixtures to the butter mixture in two batches, starting and ending with the flour mixture. Scrape down the bowl after each addition.

7. Gradually pour in the coffee. Scrape down the bowl and beat until thoroughly combined.

8. Divide the cake batter evenly among the cake pans or muffin tins. For 9-inch cake pans and half-sheet pans, bake 30 to 45 minutes, or until a toothpick comes out clean; for cupcakes, bake 20 to 25 minutes, or until they spring back after being touched.

9. Allow the cake to cool for 20 minutes. Once the cake is cool, release it from its pan by running a metal spatula or knife along the sides of the pan. Flip the cake over onto another pan or cake board and peel away the layer of parchment.

HOT TIPS

* Cakes can be stored in the freezer for up to 5 days, tightly wrapped in at least two layers of plastic wrap.

* If you are concerned about caffeine, omit the coffee and replace it with 1⅛ cups (5 ounces) milk plus 1⅛ cups (5 ounces) water.

* If you are concerned about nut allergies, double the vanilla extract and omit the almond extract.

Yellow Cake

YIELD: three 9-inch rounds, 1 half-sheet (13 x 18 inches), or 24 cupcakes

This yellow cake is an all-time kid favorite thanks to its neutral— but still delicious—flavor. It's moist and has a looser crumb than a traditional white cake, but it's still great for sculpting. For kids we most often pair this cake with Chocolate Buttercream (page 71). That simple combination is always a huge hit.

WHAT YOU NEED

2¾ cups (10 ounces) all-purpose flour

1 tablespoon baking powder

1 cup (2 sticks; 8 ounces) unsalted butter

2 cups (14 ounces) granulated sugar

1½ teaspoons pure vanilla extract

4 eggs

1 cup (8 ounces) milk

METHOD

1. Preheat the oven to 350°F. Brush the bottoms and sides of the pans with melted butter and line the bottoms with parchment paper.

2. In a large bowl, sift together the flour and baking powder. Set aside.

3. In the bowl of a standing mixer fitted with a paddle attachment, combine the butter and sugar and beat on medium speed until light and fluffy.

4. Set the mixer to low speed and add the vanilla, then the eggs, one at a time, scraping thoroughly between additions.

5. Alternately add the flour mixer and the milk to the butter mixture in three batches, starting with the flour. Scrape down the bowl between additions and beat until thoroughly combined. Set the mixer to medium speed for about 20 seconds then stop and scrape the sides of the bowl.

6. Divide the batter evenly among the cake pans or muffin tins. For 9-inch cake pans and half-sheet pans, bake 30 to 45 minutes, or until a toothpick comes out clean; for cupcakes, bake 20 to 25 minutes, or until they spring back after being touched.

7. Allow the cake to cool for 20 minutes. Once the cake is cool, release it from its pan by running a metal spatula or knife along the sides of the pan. Flip the cake over onto another pan or cake board and peel away the layer of parchment.

HOT TIP

* Cakes can be stored in the freezer for up to 5 days, tightly wrapped in at least two layers of plastic wrap.

Apple Cinnamon Cake

YIELD: three 9-inch rounds, 1 half-sheet (13 x 18 inches), or 24 cupcakes

Baking this cake fills the kitchen with the most wonderful aroma. It's delicious for any fall occasion. Use your favorite tart, firm apples — we like to use a mix of varieties because it gives such nice flavor. We usually include Granny Smiths, and when Crispins are in season we use those, too. This cake is fantastic with our Brown Sugar Buttercream (page 75).

WHAT YOU NEED

3¾ cups (16 ounces) all-purpose flour

1 tablespoon plus 1 teaspoon baking powder

1 tablespoon plus 1 teaspoon cinnamon

1 teaspoon baking soda

1 teaspoon salt

½ teaspoon ground cloves

1 cup (8 ounces; 2 sticks) unsalted butter

3 cups (21 ounces) packed brown sugar

4 eggs

1 cup (8 ounces) unsweetened applesauce

2 apples, peeled and chopped into ½-inch pieces

METHOD

1. Preheat the oven to 350°F. Brush the bottoms and sides of the pans with melted butter and line the bottoms with parchment paper.

2. In a large bowl, sift together the flour, baking powder, cinnamon, baking soda, salt, and cloves. Set aside.

3. In the bowl of a standing mixer fitted with a paddle attachment, combine the butter and brown sugar and beat on medium speed until light and fluffy.

4. Set the mixer to low speed and add the eggs, one at a time, scraping thoroughly after each addition.

5. Alternately add the flour mixture and the applesauce to the butter mixture in three batches, starting with the flour. Scrape down the bowl after each addition and beat until thoroughly combined. Set the mixer to medium speed for about 20 seconds, then stop and scrape the sides of the bowl.

6. Add the apples and stir them in just until they are incorporated.

7. Divide the batter evenly among the cake pans or muffin tins. For 9-inch cake pans and half-sheet pans, bake 30 to 45 minutes, or until a toothpick comes out clean; for cupcakes, bake 20 to 25 minutes, or until they spring back after being touched.

8. Allow the cake to cool for 20 minutes. Once the cake is cool, release it from its pan by running a metal spatula or knife along the sides of the pan. Flip the cake over onto another pan or cake board and peel away the layer of parchment.

HOT TIP

* Cakes can be stored in the freezer for up to 5 days, tightly wrapped in at least two layers of plastic wrap.

Gingerbread Cake

YIELD: three 9-inch rounds, 1 half-sheet (13 x 18 inches), or 24 cupcakes

The flavors of gingerbread — ginger, cloves, cinnamon, and nutmeg — meet in a moist, mouthwatering cake that has a gorgeous dark molasses color. People love this cake because it's unexpected and they can't believe how good it is, especially when it's paired with cream cheese frosting, a variation of Vanilla Buttercream (page 71). I love to make this around the holidays and all through the winter.

WHAT YOU NEED

3¾ cups (16 ounces) all-purpose flour

1 tablespoon plus 1½ teaspoons ground ginger

1 tablespoon baking powder

1 teaspoon salt

1 tablespoon cinnamon

¾ teaspoon ground cloves

¾ teaspoon ground nutmeg

1½ cups (12 ounces) boiling water

1½ teaspoons baking soda

¾ cup plus 1 tablespoon (6½ ounces) unsalted butter

1 cup (7 ounces) packed brown sugar

3 eggs

1½ cups (12 ounces) molasses

METHOD

1. Preheat the oven to 350°F. Brush the bottoms and sides of the pans with melted butter and line the bottoms with parchment paper.

2. In a large bowl, sift together the flour, ginger, baking powder, salt, cinnamon, cloves, and nutmeg. Set aside.

3. In a medium bowl, stir together the boiling water and the baking soda.

4. In the bowl of a standing mixer fitted with a paddle attachment, combine the butter and brown sugar and beat on medium speed until light and fluffy.

5. Set the mixer to low speed and add the eggs, one at a time, and then the molasses, scraping thoroughly after each addition.

6. Alternately add the flour mixture and the baking soda mixture to the butter mixture in three batches, starting with the flour. Scrape down the bowl after each addition and beat until thoroughly combined. Set the mixer to medium speed for about 15 seconds, then stop and scrape the sides of the bowl.

7. Divide the batter evenly among the cake pans or muffin tins. For 9-inch cake pans and half-sheet pans, bake 30 to 45 minutes, or until a toothpick comes out clean; for cupcakes, bake 20 minutes, or until they spring back after being touched.

8. Allow the cake to cool for 20 minutes. Once the cake is cool, release it from its pan by running a metal spatula or knife along the sides of the pan. Flip the cake over onto another pan or cake board and peel away the layer of parchment.

HOT TIP

* Cakes can be stored in the freezer for up to 5 days, tightly wrapped in at least two layers of plastic wrap.

Carrot Cake

YIELD: three 9-inch rounds, 1 half-sheet (13 x 18 inches), or 24 cupcakes

Carrot cake aficionados have told us this is one of the best recipes they've ever tasted. It's a little bit lighter than our other cakes, and equally delicious. It's so moist and yet firm enough to be sculpted, unlike most carrot cakes. It works well with all the projects in this book, and it's delicious with the cream cheese variation of our Vanilla Buttercream (page 71). The recipe calls for chopped walnuts; always chop nuts before weighing and measuring.

WHAT YOU NEED

- 3 cups (12 ounces) cake flour
- 2 teaspoons cinnamon
- 1¼ teaspoons salt
- 1¼ teaspoons baking powder
- 5 eggs
- 3 cups (21 ounces) granulated sugar
- 2 cups (16 ounces) vegetable oil
- 2¼ cups (15 ounces) shredded carrots
- 1½ cups (6 ounces) chopped walnuts

METHOD

1. Preheat the oven to 350°F. Brush the bottoms and sides of the pans with melted butter and line the bottoms with parchment paper.

2. In a large bowl, sift together the flour, cinnamon, salt, and baking powder. Set aside.

3. In the bowl of a standing mixer fitted with a whip attachment, combine the eggs and sugar and beat them on medium speed for 1 minute, then on high speed until they are 3 times their original volume, about 4 minutes longer.

4. Set the mixer to low speed and add the oil slowly, and beat until combined.

5. With the mixer still set to low speed, gradually add the flour mixture to the egg mixture until just combined, being careful not to overmix.

6. Gently stir in carrots and walnuts.

7. Divide the batter evenly among the cake pans or muffin tins. For 9-inch cake pans and half-sheet pans, bake 30 to 45 minutes, or until a toothpick comes out clean; for cupcakes, bake 20 to 25 minutes, or until they spring back after being touched.

8. Allow the cake to cool for 20 minutes. Once the cake is cool, release it from its pan by running a metal spatula or knife along the sides of the pan. Flip the cake over onto another pan or cake board and peel away the layer of parchment.

HOT TIP

* Cakes can be stored in the freezer for up to 5 days, tightly wrapped in at least two layers of plastic wrap.

Lemon Cake

YIELD: three 9-inch rounds, 1 half sheet (13 x 18 inches), or 24 cupcakes

This recipe uses only egg whites, not whole eggs, and the resulting cake is magically light and fluffy. The fresh lemon flavor is perfect for any springtime event. I love pairing it with our Lemon Curd Buttercream (page 73), or simply having a slice of it with fresh fruit.

WHAT YOU NEED

2 cups (8 ounces) cake flour

1½ cups plus 1½ teaspoons (9 ounces) all-purpose flour

2¼ teaspoons baking powder

1 cup (8 ounces; 2 sticks) unsalted butter

3 cups (21 ounces) granulated sugar

1 tablespoon pure vanilla extract

1½ teaspoons lemon zest

1 tablespoon lemon juice

¾ teaspoon salt

1 cup (8 ounces; about 7 eggs) egg whites or pasteurized egg whites in liquid form

1½ cups (12 ounces) milk

METHOD

1. Preheat the oven to 350°F. Brush the bottoms and sides of the pans with melted butter and line the bottoms with parchment paper.

2. In a large bowl, sift together the cake flour, all-purpose flour, and baking powder. Set aside.

3. In the bowl of a standing mixer fitted with a paddle attachment, combine the butter and sugar and beat on medium speed until light and fluffy.

4. Add the vanilla, lemon zest, lemon juice, and salt.

5. Set the mixer to low speed and gradually add the egg whites, scraping often.

6. Alternately add the flour mixture and the milk to the butter mixture in two batches, starting with the flour. Scrape down the bowl between additions and beat until thoroughly combined. Set the mixer to medium-high speed for about 20 seconds, then stop and scrape the sides of the bowl.

7. Divide the batter evenly among the cake pans or muffin tins. For 9-inch cake pans and half-sheet pans, bake 30 to 45 minutes, or until a toothpick comes out clean; for cupcakes, bake 20 to 25 minutes, or until they spring back after being touched.

8. Allow the cake to cool for 20 minutes. Once the cake is cool, release it from its pan by running a metal spatula or knife along the sides of the pan. Flip the cake over onto another pan or cake board and peel away the layer of parchment.

HOT TIP

* Cakes can be stored in the freezer for up to 5 days, tightly wrapped in at least two layers of plastic wrap.

Servings

Use this chart to help you determine how many servings you'll get from different sizes of cake. With sculpted cakes you will have to start with a larger size cake, because as you sculpt, it gets smaller. So keep the number of people you want to serve in mind as you're deciding what size cakes to bake. The numbers tell you how many servings per size and shape of cake. Obviously, the number of servings depends on the size of the slice — and in my family that depends on whether my dad or mom is cutting! This chart assumes slices are approximately 1 inch wide and 4 inches high.

	NO. OF SERVINGS BY CAKE SHAPE		
CAKE SIZE	ROUND CAKE	SQUARE CAKE	PETAL CAKE
6-inch	6	10	5
8-inch	18	25	10
10-inch	30	40	25
12-inch	45	50	40
14-inch	60	75	55
16-inch	80	100	75

Vanilla Buttercream

YIELD: 8 cups (enough to fill and crumb coat two 9-inch round cakes, each consisting of two layers of filling and three layers of cake; or 24 cupcakes with swirls)

If you make cakes often, you will start to think of this as your go-to buttercream: smooth and delicious and just sweet, strong, and stable enough to fill sculpted and tiered cakes or look gorgeous on top of cupcakes. You can mix it up with all kinds of variations — we've included some of our favorites here.

WHAT YOU NEED

2¾ cups plus 3 tablespoons (20 ounces) granulated sugar

1¼ cups (10 ounces) egg whites, or pasteurized egg whites in liquid form

2½ cups (20 ounces; 5 sticks) unsalted butter, cubed and softened

¼ cup plus 2 tablespoons (2½ ounces) pure vanilla extract

METHOD

1. In the bowl of a standing mixer, thoroughly whisk together the sugar and egg whites.

2. Set the bowl over a pot of boiling water. Whisking constantly, heat the mixture until all the sugar crystals have dissolved and the mixture is hot. Get it as hot as you can but be careful not to cook the egg whites.

3. Put the bowl back in the mixer fitted with a whip attachment. Beat on high speed until the mixture forms a stiff meringue and the bottom comes to room temperature, about 10 minutes.

4. Stop the mixer and replace the whip attachment with the paddle attachment.

5. Set the mixer to low speed and add the butter, a few cubes at a time. When all the butter is incorporated, turn the mixer to medium speed and mix until fluffy.

6. Set the mixer to low speed and add the vanilla. Once the vanilla is incorporated, scrape the bowl and continue to mix on medium speed until you have a smooth, creamy texture. If the buttercream is too liquid, refrigerate until completely cool and stiff, then rewhip.

7. You can use the buttercream immediately, store it in an airtight container at room temperature for up to 2 days, or refrigerate it in an airtight container for up to 10 days.

VARIATIONS

Add the ingredients for these variations after step 6 in the original recipe. Be sure that the buttercream is cool and stiff before adding any variations.

CHOCOLATE: Add ½ cup (4 ounces) cooled melted semisweet (58 percent cocoa) chocolate in a steady stream while mixing on low speed. Be sure that the chocolate is cool or it will melt the buttercream.

MOCHA: Add ¼ cup (2 ounces) cold strong coffee and ¼ cup (2 ounces) cooled, melted semisweet (58 percent cocoa) chocolate in a slow steady stream while mixing on low speed.

RASPBERRY: Add ½ cup (4 ounces) seedless raspberry puree and mix on low speed.

CREAM CHEESE: Add 1 cup (8 ounces) softened cream cheese and mix on low speed.

HOT TIPS

* To eliminate any grease or oil that could prevent the meringue from whipping to its proper volume, clean all utensils and equipment with a paper towel moistened with lemon juice.

* After you refrigerate the buttercream, reconstitute it by heating one-third of the buttercream in the microwave until it is warm to the touch. Place the remaining two-thirds in the bowl of a mixer and beat on medium speed. Add the warmed buttercream and beat until creamy.

* We use a fair amount of vanilla extract in our Vanilla Buttercream, which gives it an ivory color. If you want a lighter shade, use either clear vanilla extract or less of the dark vanilla extract, keeping in mind that this will affect the flavor.

* If the buttercream is too loose or separating, the butter may not be of high enough quality. Use good quality butter, with a high fat content. If that isn't the problem, your work area may be too warm. Chill the buttercream in the refrigerator for at least 15 minutes, then rewhip it with a paddle.

Peanut Butter Buttercream

YIELD: 8 cups (enough to fill and crumb-coat two 9-inch round cakes, each consisting of two layers of filling and three layers of cake; or 24 cupcakes with swirls)

Kids everywhere adore peanut butter — and so do most adults I know — so we turned this favorite food into a delicious, creamy frosting and filling. The method is similar to the one used to make our Vanilla Buttercream (page 71), and the result is scrumptious. Of course I love this with our Chocolate Cake (page 64).

WHAT YOU NEED

2¼ cups (15 ounces) granulated sugar

1¼ cups (10 ounces) egg whites, or pasteurized egg whites in liquid form

2½ cups (20 ounces; 5 sticks) unsalted butter, cubed and softened

2 tablespoons (1 ounce) pure vanilla extract

⅓ cup plus 1 tablespoon (3½ ounces) peanut butter

METHOD

1. In the bowl of a standing mixer, thoroughly whisk together the sugar and egg whites.

2. Set the bowl over a pot of boiling water. Whisking constantly, heat the mixture until all the sugar crystals have dissolved and the mixture is hot. Get it as hot as you can, being careful not to cook the eggs.

3. Put the bowl back in the mixer fitted with a whip attachment. Beat on high speed until the mixture forms a stiff meringue and the bottom comes to room temperature, about 10 minutes.

4. Stop the mixer and replace the whip attachment with the paddle attachment.

5. Set the mixer to low speed and add the butter, a few cubes at a time. When all the butter is incorporated, turn the mixer to medium speed and mix until fluffy.

6. Set the mixer to low speed and add the vanilla. Once the vanilla is incorporated, scrape the bowl.

7. Add the peanut butter and mix it in on low speed. Scrape the bowl and continue to beat on medium speed until you have a smooth, creamy texture. If the buttercream is too liquid, refrigerate until completely cool and stiff, then rewhip.

8. You can use the buttercream immediately, store it in an airtight container at room temperature for up to 2 days, or refrigerate it in an airtight container for up to 10 days.

Lemon Curd Buttercream

YIELD: 8 cups (enough to fill and crumb-coat two 9-inch round cakes, each consisting of two layers of filling and three layers of cake; or 24 cupcakes with swirls)

Lemon lovers adore this buttercream. The lemon flavor, which comes from the addition of a rich lemon curd, is just right. Use this with our Lemon Cake (page 69) for a double dose of sweet citrus or with our Yellow Cake (page 65) for a nice balance of flavor.

WHAT YOU NEED

2 cups (14 ounces) granulated sugar

¾ cups plus 2 tablespoons (7 ounces) egg whites, or pasteurized egg whites in liquid form

1¾ cups (14 ounces; 3½ sticks) unsalted butter, cubed and softened

¼ cup (2 ounces) pure vanilla extract

2 cups cooled Lemon Curd (page 74)

METHOD

1. In the bowl of a standing mixer, thoroughly whisk together the sugar and egg whites.

2. Set the bowl over a pot of boiling water. Whisking constantly, heat the mixture until all the sugar crystals have dissolved and the mixture is hot. Get it as hot as you can but be careful not to cook the eggs.

3. Put the bowl back in the mixer fitted with a whip attachment. Beat on high speed until the mixture forms a stiff meringue and the bottom comes to room temperature, about 10 minutes.

4. Stop the mixer and replace the whip attachment with the paddle attachment.

5. Set the mixer to low speed and add the butter, a few cubes at a time. When all the butter is incorporated, turn the mixer to medium speed and mix until fluffy.

6. Set the mixer to low speed and add the vanilla and lemon curd. Once they are incorporated, scrape the bowl and continue to mix on medium speed until you have a smooth, creamy texture. If the buttercream is too liquid, refrigerate until completely cool and stiff, then rewhip.

7. You can use the buttercream immediately, store it in an airtight container at room temperature for up to 2 days, or refrigerate it in an airtight container for up to 10 days.

HOT TIP

* If you want lemon frosting but don't have time to make lemon curd, use our Vanilla Buttercream recipe (page 71) and after step 6, add ½ cup (4 ounces) lemon juice and 2 tablespoons (1 ounce) vanilla extract. Be sure that the buttercream is cool and stiff before adding the juice and vanilla.

Lemon Curd

YIELD: 4 cups (enough for two recipes of Lemon Curd Buttercream)

Homemade lemon curd adds excellent, zippy lemon flavor to our Lemon Curd Buttercream. This is a wonderful filling for fruit tarts and a great accompaniment to fruit salad. I also love to put it on the side of a slice of cake. Use fresh lemon juice for this recipe — you can get most of it from the lemons you use for zesting.

WHAT YOU NEED

Zest of 6 lemons

1 cup plus 2 tablespoons (9 ounces) lemon juice

2½ cups (18 ounces) granulated sugar

6 large eggs

2 cups (16 ounces; 4 sticks) unsalted butter, cubed

METHOD

1. In a large metal bowl, combine the lemon zest, lemon juice, and sugar.

2. Prepare an ice bath: combine ice cubes and cold water in a bowl large enough to hold your mixing bowl. Leave enough room to add the mixing bowl without spilling the ice water.

3. Whisk the eggs into the lemon mixture and set the bowl over a pot of boiling water. Stir constantly until the curd starts to thicken, about 10 minutes.

4. Strain the curd through a mesh strainer into another large heat-resistant bowl. Add the butter a few cubes at a time and whisk until smooth.

5. Place the bowl in the ice bath and chill. Stir frequently to speed up the cooling process. Do not use in the buttercream recipe until completely cool.

6. Once the curd is cool, keep it in the refrigerator in an airtight container. It will keep in the refrigerator for up to 5 days.

Brown Sugar Buttercream

YIELD: 8 cups (enough to fill and crumb-coat two 9-inch round cakes, each consisting of two layers of filling and three layers of cake; or 24 cupcakes with swirls)

This addictive buttercream is sweetened with brown sugar instead of granulated sugar, and the result is a creamy caramel flavor. I especially love it with our Apple Cinnamon Cake (page 66). For even deeper flavor, replace the light brown sugar with dark brown sugar.

WHAT YOU NEED

3 cups plus 2 tablespoons (22 ounces) packed light brown sugar

1 cup (8 ounces) egg whites, or pasteurized egg whites in liquid form

3 cups (24 ounces; 6 sticks) unsalted butter, cubed and softened

1 tablespoon plus 2 teaspoons pure vanilla extract

METHOD

1. In the bowl of a standing mixer, thoroughly whisk together the brown sugar and egg whites.

2. Set the bowl over a pot of boiling water. Whisking constantly, heat the mixture until all the sugar crystals have dissolved and the mixture is hot. Get it as hot as you can but be careful not to cook the eggs.

3. Put the bowl back in the mixer fitted with a whip attachment. Beat on high speed until the mixture forms a stiff meringue and the bottom comes to room temperature, about 10 minutes.

4. Stop the mixer and replace the whip attachment with the paddle attachment.

5. Set the mixer to low speed and add the butter, a few cubes at a time. When all the butter is incorporated, turn the mixer to medium speed and mix until fluffy.

6. Set the mixer to low speed and add the vanilla. Once the vanilla is incorporated, scrape the bowl and continue to mix on medium speed until you have a smooth, creamy texture. If the buttercream is too liquid, refrigerate until completely cool and stiff, then rewhip.

7. You can use the buttercream immediately, store it in an airtight container at room temperature for up to 2 days, or refrigerate it in an airtight container for up to 10 days.

Cupcake Frosting

YIELD: 9½ cups (enough to frost 24 cupcakes generously)

This delicious vanilla-flavored frosting is for anyone with a sweet tooth. That's why it's one of my family's favorites! It's a wonderful topping for our cupcakes and brownies, as it picks up food coloring easily and holds colors well. However, we don't recommend it for filling sculpted cakes because it doesn't have a firm enough structure to hold the cake up.

WHAT YOU NEED

1 cup (8 ounces; 2 sticks) unsalted butter

8 cups (28 ounces) confectioners' sugar

½ cup (4 ounces) milk

2 teaspoons pure vanilla extract

METHOD

1. In the bowl of a mixer fitted with a paddle attachment, beat the butter on medium speed until smooth.

2. Turn the mixer to low speed and add 1 cup of the confectioners' sugar and beat until combined. Scrape the bowl thoroughly.

3. In a small bowl, combine the milk and vanilla. Add to the butter-sugar mixture. Set the mixer to medium speed and beat until light and fluffy.

4. Gradually add the remaining confectioners' sugar, adding as much as you need to achieve a smooth and stiff consistency.

5. Use immediately, store in an airtight container at room temperature for up to 2 days, or refrigerate for up to 10 days.

Milk Chocolate Ganache

YIELD: 4 cups (enough to fill one 9-inch round cake consisting of two layers of filling and three layers of cake, 12 regular cupcakes, or 24 mini cupcakes)

Milk chocolate ganache is a kid-friendly version of dark chocolate ganache, a rich cake filling or frosting that reminds me of the inside of a chocolate truffle. It should be smooth and creamy, and you can adjust the thickness by changing the ratio of chocolate to cream. Using the best quality chocolate you can find is especially important in this recipe, which has only two ingredients.

WHAT YOU NEED

16 ounces milk chocolate, chopped

½ cup plus 3 tablespoons (5½ ounces) heavy cream

METHOD

1. Place the chocolate in a metal or ovenproof glass bowl. Set aside.

2. Heat the heavy cream in a saucepan over medium-high heat, stirring frequently, until it starts to boil. Be careful because cream boils quickly and can boil over if you leave it for a few seconds.

3. Immediately remove the cream from the heat and pour over the chocolate. Let the mixture stand for 2 to 3 minutes.

4. Gently stir the mixture with a whisk until the chocolate is completely melted and there are no noticeable traces of cream.

5. Allow the ganache to sit at room temperature to cool and thicken.

6. When the ganache is cool, store it in an airtight container. Ganache can be kept for 2 days at room temperature or for up to 10 days refrigerated.

HOT TIP

* To reconstitute refrigerated ganache, heat it in a double boiler over very low heat to prevent burning. Heating gently makes it easier to control the consistency of the ganache for filling a cake.

Royal Icing

YIELD: 4½ cups

For cake and cookie decorators, Royal Icing is indispensable. Think of it as sweet, edible "glue" that holds together or attaches finished tiers of cake, ices cookies, creates decorations, and allows you to attach decorations directly onto the cake. The amount of sugar you use will determine the thickness of your Royal Icing. For stiffer icing, add more sugar. For looser icing (for flooding your designs), add a few drops of water to thin the icing a bit.

WHAT YOU NEED

⅓ cup (3 ounces) pasteurized egg whites

4½ cups plus 1 tablespoon (16 ounces) sifted confectioners' sugar

½ teaspoon lemon juice

METHOD

1. In the bowl of an electric mixer fitted with a paddle attachment, beat the egg whites on medium speed until soft peaks form.

2. Set the mixer to medium-low speed and gradually add the confectioners' sugar, ½ cup (4 ounces) at a time. Scrape thoroughly between additions.

3. Add the lemon juice and beat on medium-high speed until stiff peaks form and the icing is no longer shiny, 6 to 8 minutes.

4. Use immediately or place the icing in an airtight container. You can keep Royal Icing in the refrigerator for up to 5 days.

HOT TIPS

* Allow Royal Icing to come to room temperature before you use it. It will be much easier to mix and pipe.

* If you are making this for someone who might be allergic to eggs, use a mixture of 2 tablespoons plus 2 teaspoons (1½ ounces) meringue powder and ½ cup (4 ounces) water to replace the egg whites. Follow the rest of the recipe as given.

Simple Syrup

YIELD: 2 cups (enough to brush 48 cupcakes or a large tiered cake)

We use simple syrup to add another touch of a sweet flavor to cakes, and to make them extra-moist. This is a basic recipe for the simplest of sweet syrups. When it's cool, you can add an extract or citrus juice that would go well with your cake. We brush a layer of flavored simple syrups onto our cakes before filling them with buttercream.

WHAT YOU NEED

1 cup (7 ounces) granulated sugar

1 cup (8 ounces) water

METHOD

1. Combine the sugar and water in a medium saucepan. Stir with a whisk to hydrate the sugar completely.

2. Without stirring, bring the mixture to a boil over high heat. Remove from the heat and allow to cool.

3. When cool, the simple syrup can be stored in an airtight container in the refrigerator for up to 2 weeks.

4. To use, brush the syrup on the tops of cakes before placing the filling.

HOT TIP

* When you add flavor to simple syrup, the amount you add depends on how strong you want it to be. For this recipe, start with about ¼ cup (2 ounces) of juice or extract — you can add more for greater intensity of flavor.

Rolled Fondant

YIELD: 2 pounds (enough to cover one 10-inch round, 4-inch high cake)

Rolled fondant is a smooth dough that we use to cover cakes, cupcakes, and cookies to give a beautiful, smooth finish. At Confetti Cakes, we buy fondant by the tub. It's one of the few things we don't make from scratch, because I find that prefabricated fondant has a higher quality and usually a finer taste than what you can make at home. You can purchase fondant in many flavors; we like chocolate and vanilla (see Resources, page 217). You can even find kosher rolled fondant. If you cannot find fondant in a store near you, or you don't have time to order it online, or you want to experiment with making it yourself, try this fairly simple recipe.

WHAT YOU NEED

3 tablespoons cold water

1 tablespoon unflavored gelatin

½ cup (4 ounces) light corn syrup

1½ tablespoons glycerin

1 tablespoon pure vanilla extract

9 cups plus 2 tablespoons (32 ounces) confectioners' sugar, sifted

METHOD

1. In a small bowl, combine the cold water and gelatin. Allow the mixture to sit for 2 minutes.

2. Place the gelatin mixture in a double boiler and melt over low heat. Remove from the heat and stir in the corn syrup, glycerin, and vanilla.

3. Place 6 cups of the confectioners' sugar in the bowl of an electric mixer fitted with a paddle attachment. With the mixer on low speed, pour the gelatin mixture into the confectioners' sugar. Turn to medium speed and beat until a sticky ball forms.

4. Using a spatula coated with shortening, scrape the dough onto a clean surface and knead in the remaining sugar until the fondant is smooth.

5. Wrap the fondant in several layers of plastic and store in an airtight container at room temperature for at least 24 hours before using.

HOT TIPS

* Do not get rolled fondant wet. It gets sticky and becomes difficult to use.

* In hot climates or in the summer, you may need to use a little extra confectioners' sugar. If possible, work in an air conditioned area.

* Do not refrigerate fondant-covered cakes. Fondant does not like humidity so if it's refrigerated, it will start to sweat when it comes out of the refrigerator.

* A fondant-covered cake will keep for 2 days without refrigeration. Store it in a cool and dry area.

* For flavor variations, substitute 1 tablespoon of another extract such as lemon, almond, or mint for the vanilla.

How Much Fondant?

This chart can help you determine approximately how much fondant you will need to cover cakes that are 4 inches high. If you are using fondant for the first time or you are a beginner, start off using more fondant than called for — it is easier to learn with too much fondant than too little.

CAKE SIZE	ROUND CAKE AND PETAL SHAPED CAKES	SQUARE CAKES
4-inch	¾ pound	1 pound
6-inch	1 pound	1½ pounds
8-inch	1½ pounds	2 pounds
10-inch	2 pounds	3 pounds
12-inch	3 pounds	4 pounds
14-inch	4 pounds	5 pounds
16-inch	5 pounds	6 pounds

MEASURING GUM PASTE, FONDANT, AND MARZIPAN WITHOUT A SCALE

If you do not have a scale, use this chart to approximate the amount needed.

AMOUNT	APPROXIMATE SIZE
¼ ounce	a small marble
½ ounce	a large gumball
1 ounce	a golf ball
4 ounces	a racquet ball
6 ounces	a tennis ball
8 ounces	an orange

Cookies

. . . .

Kids love just about all cookies, but with the fun, whimsical, colorfully decorated cookies that you'll find in this chapter, kids won't be able to contain their enthusiasm. And they'll love them even more if they get to help in the cookie-making process! Whether you make sparkly stars, swirled lollipops, playful farm animals, or sassy gingerbread kids in Hawaiian attire, they are guaranteed to be a hit with young audiences — and grown-ups, too!

In addition to being fabulous to display and delicious to eat, cookies are a perfect way to get started in pastry decoration. You'll learn how to work with icing and pipe sweet designs. From gum paste and fondant you can create fabulous decorations for projects that are simpler to complete than sculpted cakes. And you can use what you learn from making the cookies in this chapter to inspire your imagination and make whatever kind of cookie you like! The basic cookie doughs in this book (vanilla, chocolate, gingerbread; see pages 60–63) will work with almost any shape you can imagine. You can cut shapes with cookie cutters (if you do that, you can always trim the shapes with an X-acto knife to make them more precise) or cut shapes by hand with an X-acto knife, working from a template in this book or a drawing from your own imagination.

Keep in mind that while cookies aren't as time-consuming as large cakes, planning ahead is still important. Especially if you want to make a large quantity of cookies, I suggest allowing two days for the project — one for baking (giving yourself time to chill the dough in the freezer after you roll it into sheets, and then chill it again after you've cut the cookies from the dough, **before** putting them in the oven), and one for decorating. Always leave time for the icing to dry, and for more involved cookies you might even want to ice your cookies on one day and let the icing set overnight before adding decorative details. Sugar decorations are best made in advance, too, so they have ample time to harden before you attach them to your cookies.

Star Cookies

YIELD: Approximately 24 cookies

I **love the magic of stars.** In red, white, and blue, these cookies are perfect for a Fourth of July barbecue. Change the colors to red, gold, and green and you have a dynamic dessert for a Christmas party — or go with blue, white, and silver for a Hannukah feast. Decorate them with pastels or bright purples, and you have the perfect cookies for a princess or a magician-in-the-making. Mixing the colors and patterns makes every cookie special.

WHAT YOU NEED

RECIPES

1 recipe cookie dough
(see Basic Recipes, pages 60–63)

1 recipe Royal Icing (page 78)

MATERIALS

Food-coloring gels: super red, delphinium blue

Sanding sugar in various colors (here we used white, red, and blue)

Metallic dust (optional)

Lemon extract (optional)

EQUIPMENT

Star cookie cutters
or templates (page 106)

Toothpicks

Small offset spatula

Pastry bags and plastic couplers

Pastry tips: #2, #3

Scissors

Small rubber spatula

Small bowl

Spoon(s)

Small paintbrush (optional)

TECHNIQUES

Dyeing Royal Icing (page 25)

Filling a pastry bag (page 26)

Flooding (page 28)

Decorating with sanding sugar
(page 30)

Piping dots and lines (page 27)

Overpiping (page 30)

Painting with dusts (page 50)

1 Prepare the cookie dough and roll it out as directed. Use the star cutters to cut out cookies and bake according to the recipe. While the cookies are cooling, make the Royal Icing.

2. Divide the Royal Icing into 3 portions, and dye one red and one blue. Leave the last portion white. Fill pastry bags fitted with #2 tips with some of each color you will use. For each cookie, using the shape of the cookie as your guide, pipe a complete outline of the cookie. Make sure there are no gaps in the outline or your flood will spill outside the line.

3. Add water to the remaining icing to loosen it and fill pastry bags fitted with #3 tips. Flood cookies one at a time.

4. For cookies decorated with sanding sugar, hold the flooded cookie over a bowl and spoon on the sanding sugar. (For the largest cookies you will need about 3 tablespoons of sanding sugar per cookie.) Let the cookies dry for at least 20 minutes before removing the excess sugar. If you disturb the cookies too soon, the icing may run off the sides.

5. For cookies with dots, stripes, and metallic dusts, let the cookies dry overnight and decorate the next day. Different sizes of pastry tips will give you various sizes of piped dots and stripes. To achieve a rich metallic gold color you may need to apply more than one coat.

HOT TIPS

* Mix and match the colored icings and sugars to achieve different effects. Red sanding sugar looks very different on a cookie flooded with white icing than it does on a cookie flooded with red icing.

* If an adult prepares the cookies, kids can have lots of fun drawing on them with edible food markers and painting them with gels and powders.

Lollipop Cookies

YIELD: Approximately 24 cookies

When I was a little girl, I loved looking at the bright colors of sugary lollipops, but my favorite things to eat then were cookies (and that's still true today!). These cookies feature the best of both worlds, and they are lots of fun to display for a party. If you don't have tall jars, you could keep them upright by sticking the lollipop sticks in florist foam. They also look fantastic arranged on a plate. These designs work on just about any shape of cookie — all you need is the drop-in flooding technique. If you don't have a set of round cookie cutters, you can create a variety of circle templates by tracing small jars or other round objects in your kitchen.

WHAT YOU NEED

RECIPES

1 recipe cookie dough (see Basic Recipes, pages 60–63)

1 recipe Royal Icing (page 78)

MATERIALS

Food-coloring gels: lemon yellow, sunset orange, super red, avocado, royal blue, violet, rose pink

White lollipop sticks, $\frac{3}{16}$ inch thick and 12 inches long, cut into varied lengths

EQUIPMENT

Toothpicks

Small offset spatula

Scissors

Round cutters: 1½-inch, 1⅞-inch, 2⅛-inch, 2½-inch, 2⅞-inch

Pastry bags and plastic couplers

Pastry tips: #2, #3

TECHNIQUES

Dyeing Royal Icing (page 25)

Filling a pastry bag (page 26)

Flooding (page 28)

Drop-in flooding (page 29)

METHOD

1. Prepare the cookie dough and roll it out as directed, **except for the thickness. For this project you will need to roll the dough slightly thicker than ¼ inch, depending on the size of your lollipop stick.** The dough should be about twice as thick as the stick. So for a ³⁄₁₆ inch-thick stick roll the dough ⅜ inch thick. Use the round cutters to cut out cookies and then insert the sticks into the edges of the cookies, halfway into the circles. Bake according to the recipe, checking for doneness and possibly baking for 1 to 2 minutes longer due to the extra thickness. **I suggest test-baking one cookie before baking the entire batch to make sure the dough is thick enough and the stick does not show through the cookie.** Let the cookies cool completely. While the cookies are cooling, make the Royal Icing.

2. Divide the icing, and dye each portion in the colors you will use. Prepare stiff and loose icing in each color. Put the stiff icings in pastry bags fitted with #2 tips and the loose icings in bags fitted with #3 tips. Using the shapes of the cookie as your guide, pipe a complete outline on each cookie using stiff icing.

3. For the drop-in flooding, flood and decorate one cookie at a time, using looser icing. Have all your colors ready and close at hand. Begin by flooding an entire cookie. Without waiting for the cookie to dry, drop in the color(s) in the shape that you want.

Techniques for Cookies Pictured
(clockwise from top)
As soon as the cookie is filled with flood, drop in the following designs:

DOTS: Drop in dots using the #2 tip for smaller dots and the #3 tip for larger dots.

TEARDROPS: Drop in a dot, then pull away gently from the center with a toothpick to create a teardrop shape.

SWIRLS: Use a pastry bag fitted with a #3 tip and filled with semi-stiff icing, which is just slightly thicker than the flood icing and will hold its shape a little better. Pipe a swirl in a clockwise motion, starting in the center of the cookie and working your way outward, following the shape of the cookie.

HOT TIP

* Use these cookie lollipops to replace the lollipops in the Candy Factory Cake (page 165). Then you can have your cookies and cake all at once!

Farm Animal Cookies

YIELD: Approximately 24 cookies

Children learn the letters of the alphabet quickly with word associations. What better way to teach them their letters than with cookies? Their favorite animals can be delicious and educational at the same time. Here are a few of our favorites. Many animal cookie cutter sets come with a variety of animals to choose from (see the Resources section on page 217 for information on where to find cutters). You can pipe letters on or cut them out of gum paste as we do here. You could also add numbers (a child's age, perhaps, for a birthday) or someone's first initial.

WHAT YOU NEED

RECIPES

1 recipe cookie dough (see Basic Recipes, pages 60–63)

1 recipe Royal Icing (page 78)

MATERIALS

Food-coloring gels: sunset orange, coal black, rose pink, electric pink, electric green, royal blue, lemon yellow, buckeye brown, leaf green, super red.

Black food marker (optional, for cow)

3 ounces gum paste or fondant (optional, for letters)

Shortening (for rolling out fondant or gum paste)

Egg whites (optional)

EQUIPMENT

Animal cookie cutters, approximately 2½-inch by 3-inch, or templates (page 106–7)

X-acto knife

Toothpicks

Small offset spatula

Pastry bags and plastic couplers

Pastry tips: #1, #2, #3

Scissors

Letter cutter set, letters approximately 1 inch tall (optional)

Small rolling pin (optional)

Plastic mat (optional)

Scalpel or paring knife (optional)

1 small paintbrush (optional)

TECHNIQUES

Making a template (page 31)

Dyeing Royal Icing (page 25)

Filling a pastry bag (page 26)

Flooding (page 28)

Overpiping (page 30)

Dyeing fondant and gum paste (page 50)

METHOD

One day in advance: *Bake the cookies, outline, and flood.*

1. Prepare the cookie dough and roll it out as directed. Use the animal cutters or templates to cut out cookies. Bake according to the recipe. Let the cookies cool completely. While the cookies are cooling, make the Royal Icing.

2. Divide the Royal Icing into the correct number of portions (this will depend on how many different animals you are making) and dye all the colors you will use to outline the cookies. Leave at least one portion white in case you need it later for details.

3. Fill pastry bags fitted with #2 tips with stiff icing and outline the cookies. Add water to the remaining icing to loosen and fill pastry bags fitted with #3 tips. Flood the cookies one at a time. (See the specific instructions below for outlining and flooding the animals shown here.) Let the cookies dry, uncovered, on a flat surface overnight. They will be ready for you to add the finishing details the next day.

DECORATE THE COOKIES
Techniques for Cookies Pictured

SHEEP: Outline and flood the body of the sheep in white icing, the legs and tail in black icing, and the face in flesh color. Let dry overnight. The next day, fill a pastry bag fitted with a #1 tip with white stiff icing. Pipe a straight white line for the hooves and pipe curls all over the sheep's body. Dot the eye with stiff black icing using a #1 pastry tip. Pipe the ear with flesh-colored icing using a #2 tip.

FROG: Outline and flood the two large round eyes with white icing. Outline and flood the entire body in green, using the shape of the cookie as a guide. Let dry overnight. The next day, using a #1 tip and white icing, pipe the frog's eyes and pipe two dots for his nose. In black icing, pipe his eyes and eyelids using a #1 tip. Pipe his mouth in red icing using a #2 tip. Overpipe the outline of the body, legs, and feet in the same green color you used to outline the flood, using a #1 pastry tip and stiff icing to get a finer line. Be careful not to pipe over his eyes!

BUNNY: Outline and flood the entire cookie in white icing. Let dry overnight. The next day, overpipe the entire outline of the cookie using a #1 tip and stiff white icing. Also use the #1 tip and stiff white icing to overpipe the definition of the bunny's legs, ears, and tail. Use pale pink icing and a #2 tip to pipe a dot for the nose and to create the insides of the ears. Give the bunny an eye with a dot of black stiff icing, using a #1 tip.

PIG: Outline and flood the entire cookie with pale pink icing. With the stiff pale pink icing, create the pig's tail. Start at the backside of the pig by piping a straight line, then quickly turn your hand in a circular motion to create the curl. Let dry overnight. The next day, use stiff chocolate brown icing and a #1 tip to pipe the eye, nostrils, and hooves.

HORSE: Outline and flood the entire horse's body, including the ear, with brown icing. Let dry overnight. The next day, fill a pastry bag fitted with a #1 tip with dark chocolate brown icing and pipe the hooves, tail, mane, mouth, nose, and eye. Pipe a tiny dot of pale pink icing in the ear for an extra detail.

DUCK: Outline and flood the entire duck, except for the feet and beak, with white icing. Let dry overnight. The next day, create the wing of the duck using a #2 tip and stiff white icing. Use bright orange icing and a #1 tip to pipe the feet and beak. Give the duck an eye with a dot of black stiff icing, using a #1 tip.

COW: Outline and flood the entire shape of the cow in white icing. Use the white stiff icing to create a tail. Let dry overnight. The next day, pipe the cow's udder in pale pink using a #2 tip. Using a #1 tip and stiff black icing, pipe the end of the tail, the eye, and two straight lines for hooves. Pipe the ear in white stiff icing using a #2 tip. **We do not recommend drop-in flooding to create the cow's spots.**

Dropping an extremely saturated color such as black or red into a white background usually results in bleeding. Instead, to create the cow's spots let the white flood dry overnight, then use a black food marker to draw the spots. Do not put too much pressure on the icing or you may break the surface. Use the pale pink icing and a #2 tip to pipe the cow's nose.

Once the cookies are decorated as animals, you have the option of adding gum paste or fondant letters in contrasting colors. Dye a tiny amount of gum paste or fondant (about ⅛ ounce, or half the size of a small marble) for each color you want to use. Roll it out to approximately 1⁄16 inch thick on a plastic mat lightly coated with shortening. Use the letter cutters to cut out the letters, then use a scalpel or paring knife to trim the edges, if needed. Add the letters after all the decorations have dried. Use a small paintbrush to attach them to the cookies with a tiny amount of water or egg whites.

Hula Kid Gingerbread Cookies

YIELD: Approximately 12 cookies

Gingerbread is often associated with snowy nights and holiday themes, but we thought it would be fun to give these cookies a tropical twist. They are still terrific for a winter occasion — the reminder of warm weather will be much appreciated during gray and chilly times of year, and the design will be completely unexpected. You could also make these delightful cookies for a pool party — the ginger flavor is refreshing in the summer and delicious with lemonade!

WHAT YOU NEED

RECIPES

1 recipe gingerbread cookie dough
(page 62)

1 recipe Royal Icing (page 78)

MATERIALS

Food-coloring gels: lemon yellow, violet, electric green, sunset orange, buckeye brown, royal blue, electric pink.

EQUIPMENT

Old-fashioned gingerbread boy and girl cutters, approximately 5 inches high and 4 inches wide, or templates (page 108)

X-acto knife

Toothpicks

Small offset spatula

Pastry bags and plastic couplers

Pastry tips: #1, #2, #3, #24 star

Scissors

Small rubber spatula

TECHNIQUES

Making a template (page 31)

Dyeing Royal Icing (page 25)

Filling a pastry bag (page 26)

Flooding (page 28)

Piping dots and lines (page 27)

Overpiping (page 30)

METHOD

1. Prepare the cookie dough and roll out as directed. Use the cutters or templates to cut out cookies and bake according to the recipe. While the cookies are cooling, make the Royal Icing.

2. Divide the icing and dye each portion with the appropriate colors. (See the detailed techniques for each cookie, for information on icing consistency.) Put the stiff and loose icings in pastry bags fitted with the appropriate tips.

3. Follow the piping directions below for each kid. Feel free to mix and match patterns and colors or come up with your own! Let the cookies dry, uncovered, on a flat surface for at least 3 hours for the icing to set after flooding and before overpiping the decorations.

Techniques for Cookies Pictured

HULA BOY: Dye portions of Royal Icing the colors you want for the shorts and the body. Start with the shorts, outline them with a #2 pastry tip, and flood them with a #3 pastry tip. Then outline and flood the head, ears, body, and legs. Let dry for at least 3 hours.

Dye portions of stiff icing in the colors you want for the hair, mouth, flowers for the lei, sandals, and decorations for the shorts.

Pipe the hair and eyes with chocolate brown icing, using a #1 pastry tip. Pipe the nose and belly button in the same color you used for the body with a #1 pastry tip. Pipe the mouth in pale pink using a #1 tip. Pipe the sandals in lime green using a #1 tip. Overpipe the waistband of the shorts, the flowers, and the lines at the bottom of the shorts with bright orange icing and a #1 pastry tip.

To create the lei, use white icing and a #24 star tip. Create the flowers using the same technique you would for piping dots. Pipe them along the neck and chest to create a lei. Dot the centers of the flowers with yellow icing using a #1 tip.

HULA GIRL: Dye Royal Icing the color you want for the body. Outline the body, head, ears, and legs using a #2 pastry tip and flood it using a #3 pastry tip. (You don't need to attach the legs to the rest of the body; they will be covered by the grass skirt later on!) Let dry for at least 3 hours.

Dye portions of stiff icing in the colors you want for the grass skirt, tube top, hair, mouth, and flowers for the lei.

Pipe the grass skirt with bright green icing using a #2 pastry tip. Start at the waistline and pipe dots to create a border. Work from the bottom of the border and pipe long straight lines of varying length. When you finish one layer of "grass," continue with more strands overlapping each other. This will create a three-dimensional effect. Next outline and flood the tube top in yellow.

Pipe the hair and eyes with chocolate brown icing, using a #1 pastry tip. Overpipe the nose and belly button with the same color icing you used for the body and a #1 pastry tip. Pipe the mouth in pale pink using a #1 tip. Create the lei with lilac icing using a #24 star tip. Pipe the flowers as you would dots. Pipe them along the neck and over the tube top to create a lei, and pipe three flowers on each ankle. Dot the centers of the flowers with bright pink icing using a #1 tip.

HOT TIP

* This is literally a hot tip! If the weather is extremely humid or hot and the icing is taking a long time to dry, let the flooded cookies sit overnight before overpiping the decorations.

Easter Cookies

YIELD: Approximately 12 cookies

*T*hese cuddly creatures — in the shape of eggs perfect for any spring occasion — are so cute. Simple decorations give them tons of personality. For the cookies pictured here, we used a little sugar dough to add dimension and extra detail. We've made these for special Easter baskets and for baby showers, too!

WHAT YOU NEED

RECIPES

1 recipe cookie dough (see Basic Recipes, pages 60–63)

1 recipe Royal Icing (page 78)

MATERIALS

Food Coloring gels: Sunset orange, coal black, rose pink, electric pink, royal blue, lemon yellow, buckeye brown

Sanding sugar (optional)

3 ounces gum paste or fondant

Shortening (for rolling out fondant or gum paste)

Egg whites (optional)

EQUIPMENT

Egg cookie cutter, approximately 4 inches high and 3 inches wide, or template (page 108)

X-acto knife

Toothpicks

Small offset spatula

Pastry bags and plastic couplers

Scissors

Small rubber spatula

Pastry tips: #1, #2, #3 (for royal icing); #4, #10, #12, #804, #806, #808 (for gum paste or fondant decorations)

Small bowls (optional)

Spoon(s) (optional)

Small rolling pin

Plastic mat

Templates for sugar decorations (page 108)

Scalpel or veining tool

1 small paintbrush

Stitching tool (optional)

TECHNIQUES

Making a template (page 31)

Dyeing Royal Icing (page 25)

Filling a pastry bag (page 26)

Flooding (page 28)

Decorating with sanding sugar (optional, page 30)

Dyeing fondant and gum paste (page 50)

Overpiping (page 30)

METHOD

One day in advance: *Bake the cookies, outline, and flood.*

1. Prepare the cookie dough and roll it out as directed. Use the egg cutter or template to cut out cookies. Bake according to the recipe. Let the cookies cool completely. While the cookies are cooling, make the Royal Icing.

2. Divide the Royal Icing into 4 portions and dye one pale yellow and one pale pink. Leave one portion white. Divide the fourth portion in half; dye one half flesh-brown color for the lamb's face and the other half black for the lamb's and bunny's mouths. Put the pale yellow, pale pink, white, and flesh-brown colors into separate pastry bags fitted with #2 tips and outline the cookies (pale yellow for the chick, pale pink for the bunny, white and flesh-brown color for the lamb — for the lamb's face use the template on page 108 as a guide.)

3. Reserve a small amount of the stiff white and black icings. Add water to the remaining icings to loosen and fill pastry bags fitted with #3 tips. Flood the cookies one at a time in the same colors you used for the outlines. Let the cookies dry,

uncovered, on a flat surface overnight. The next day they will be ready for you to add the finishing details.

4. Optional: If you want to decorate any of the cookies with sanding sugar, **before the flood dries,** place the flooded cookie on a flat surface lined with parchment paper or a paper towel and spoon on the sanding sugar. You will need about 3 tablespoons of sanding sugar per cookie. Let the cookie dry for at least 20 minutes before removing the excess sugar. If you disturb the cookie too soon the icing may run off the sides.

DECORATE THE COOKIES
Techniques for Cookies Pictured

LAMB: Dye ½ ounce of fondant or gum paste (about the size of a large gumball) pale pink for the nose and inside the ears. On a plastic mat greased with shortening, roll approximately 1 ounce of white fondant or gum paste out to ¼ inch thick and cut out two ears. (Refer to template on page 108. You will need to **flip** the template to create both ears — you want a right ear *and* a left ear.)

Emboss the center of the ears with the veining tool or the back of a scalpel to make room for the pale pink inside sections of the ears. Roll out the pale pink gum paste paper-thin and cut out the center shape for each ear and the shape of the nose. With a small amount of water, attach the nose to the cookie and attach the center of each ear. Attach the ears to the top of the cookie with a small amount of stiff white icing.

Using a #1 tip and stiff white icing, pipe the curly fur of the lamb all over the face and ears. Pipe the mouth with stiff black icing and a #1 tip.

To make the eyes you need to layer four circles of gum paste. Dye a pea-size ball of gum paste black and another pea-size ball of gum paste baby blue. Roll the baby blue, black, and a marble-size ball of white gum paste paper-thin. From the white, cut out two circles, one with a #808 tip and one with a #4 tip. Then cut a circle from the baby blue with a #806 tip and a circle from the black with #804 tip. Start with the largest white circle, place the baby blue dot on top of that, then the black, and finally the smallest white and you have an eye!

For the eyebrows and eye lashes, roll a small amount of black gum paste into a tiny rope $\frac{1}{16}$ inch wide by 1 inch long. Cut two eyebrows about ¼ inch long and four eyelashes ⅛ inch long and curve them using the veining tool or a toothpick. Attach the eyes, eyelashes, and eyebrows to the cookie with tiny amounts of egg white or water, using a small brush.

BUNNY: To make the ears, follow the directions for the lamb, but reverse the colors, using pale pink for the ears themselves and white for the inside section. If you want a floppy-eared bunny, after you've attached the insides gently fold down one of the ears.

To make the nose, dye a pea-size ball of gum paste hot pink. Roll it out on a plastic mat coated with a little shortening and cut out the triangular shape. Attach the nose to the cookie with a moistened paintbrush.

Pipe the whiskers of the bunny with stiff white icing and a #1 tip and pipe the mouth with stiff black icing and a #1 tip. Create the eyes from a pea-size ball of black gum paste rolled paper-thin and cut out with a #12 tip. Attach the eyes to the cookie with a paintbrush moistened with egg whites or water.

CHICK: If you want your chick to have a fuzzy appearance, decorate it with sanding sugar before applying any other decorations. (See step 4 in the directions above.)

Start with ½ ounce of gum paste. Separate a pea-size amount from that and dye it black. Divide the remaining gum paste in half and dye one half bright orange and the other half golden yellow.

Roll the orange and yellow sections out to $\frac{1}{16}$ inch thick on a plastic mat lightly coated with shortening. Cut out the chick's beak from the bright orange and the chick's crest from the golden yellow. The beak should be about 1½ inches across and about 1 inch on all sides (see the template on page 108). Add stitching marks around the edges, then fold the beak in half. Attach the back of the beak onto the cookie with a dab of egg white, using a small paintbrush, and then place a bit of paper towel inside the beak to support it while it dries.

Cut out the crest (see the template on page 108) and use the back of a veining tool or a scalpel to make hair marks. Attach it to the top of the cookie with a dab of egg white.

To make the eyes, roll out the ball of black gum paste paper-thin and cut out circles using a #10 tip. Apply them to the chick's face with tiny dabs of egg white.

Pajama Cookies

YIELD: 6 pairs of pajamas (6 pants and 6 shirts; 12 cookies total)

These cookies are a perfect treat for a kids' sleepover! The cookies are iced and decorated with a bit of piping — and you could stop there or add adorable gum paste decorations on top. Adorning these cookies could be a fun activity for a sleepover, too. Each child could decorate his or her own pajama set. Dress the pajamas up in hearts and you have a fabulous gift for Valentine's Day. They are also wonderful to bring as a hostess gift when you or your child will be an overnight guest at the home of a friend.

WHAT YOU NEED

RECIPES

1 recipe cookie dough (see Basic Recipes, pages 60–63)

1 recipe Royal Icing (page 78)

MATERIALS

3 ounces gum paste or fondant

Food-coloring gels: lemon yellow, electric pink, royal blue, super red, avocado green, leaf green, buckeye brown, coal black

Shortening (for rolling out fondant or gum paste)

Egg whites (optional)

EQUIPMENT

Pajama cutters, shirt approximately 3 inches high and pants approximately 3½ inches high, or templates (see page 109)

X-acto knife

Scissors

Toothpicks

Pastry bags and plastic couplers

Pastry tips: #1, #2, #3 (for royal icing); #7 (for the cherry design); #3, #5, #9, #806 (for the puppy design); #10, #12 (for the smiley faces)

Plastic mat

Small rolling pin

Scalpel

Ruler

1 small paintbrush

TECHNIQUES

Making a template (page 31)

Dyeing Royal Icing (page 25)

Filling a pastry bag (page 26)

Flooding (page 28)

Piping dots and lines (page 27)

Overpiping (page 30)

Dyeing fondant and gum paste (page 50)

METHOD

One day in advance: *Bake the cookies, outline, and flood.*

1. Prepare the cookie dough and roll out as directed. Use the pajama cutters or templates to cut out cookies and bake according to the recipe. Let the cookies cool completely. While the cookies are cooling, make the Royal Icing.

2. Divide the Royal Icing into 4 portions. Dye one portion pale yellow, one hot pink, and one pale blue. Leave the last portion white. Fill pastry bags fitted with #2 tips with each color you will use. Using the shape of the cookie as your guide, pipe a complete outline of the cookie. (If you want matching pairs of pajamas, make sure you pipe matching shirts and pairs of pants for each color, but mismatched pajamas are fun, too!)

3. Reserve about ¼ of the stiff icing in each color to be used for overpiping the next day. Add water to the remaining icing to loosen and fill a pastry bag fitted with a #3 tip. Flood the cookies one at a time. Let the cookies dry, uncovered, on a flat surface overnight. The next day the cookies will be ready for you to add the finishing details.

DECORATE THE COOKIES

To create the details of the shirt and pants (i.e., collar, cuffs, and buttons), overpipe stiff icing in the same color as the flood with a #1 tip, **using the dotted lines on the template on page 109 or the photo as a guide.** Let the piped details dry for about 1 hour. While the piped details are drying, dye the fondant or gum paste for your decorations. (See the instructions for the different decorations below.) The

amount of fondant or gum paste you need depends on which design(s) you choose. Below are approximations for the decorations you'll need for one pair of pajamas (2 cookies, shirt and pants).

Techniques for Cookies Pictured

CHERRIES: Dye ¼ ounce of fondant or gum paste cherry red and ¼ ounce green for the leaves and stems. Roll both colors out, as thin as you can without tearing them, on a plastic mat covered with a little shortening. Cut out the cherries using a #7 tip. You'll need about 18 cherries for each set of pajamas.

Use a scalpel to cut 18 skinny, ½-inch-long strips from the green for the stems. Attach the stems to the cherries with a dab of egg white or water, and attach a few stems together at the top to give a variety of single and double cherries.

Cut out about 12 tiny leaf shapes (one for each cherry or cherry bunch), and attach them to the tops of the stems. Attach the cherries to the cookies with tiny dabs of egg white.

PUPPIES: The puppy faces look complicated but are really just made from a series of shapes cut out using pastry tips. Start by dyeing all the colors you will need for the face. You will need about ¼ ounce (the size of a small marble) each of light brown, white, and dark brown, and tiny (pea-size) amounts of red and black.

Roll out all the colors on a plastic mat coated in shortening. Make one head first so you understand all the parts. After that you can "mass-produce" by cutting all the shapes first, then assembling at the end. (If you are making a large quantity of cookies you may want to work with one color at a time.)

Use a #806 tip to cut the head from light brown gum paste. Cut out two cheeks from the white gum paste with a #9 pastry tip and attach them to the bottom of the head with a dab of egg white.

For the ears, cut out a circle with a #806 pastry tip from the dark brown. Cut the circle in half and round the edges and you will have two ears. Attach them to either side of the head with dabs of egg white.

From the same dark brown, cut out two eyes with a #3 tip and a nose using a #5 tip (shape it slightly into a triangle). Apply the eyes and the nose in the center of the face, where the two cheeks meet. Use the #5 tip again to cut out a small red tongue and apply it to the bottom of the face.

Once you have about 8 faces per pajama set, apply them to the cookies using tiny dabs of egg white or water. Arrange them facing in all different directions, like you might see on real fabric.

SMILEY FACES: Start with approximately ½ ounce of gum paste and dye half of it bright yellow and the other half black. Roll out the yellow onto a plastic mat coated lightly with shortening and cut out about 18 circles with a #10 tip. Roll out the black and cut out the same number of circles, this time using a #12 tip.

Attach the yellow circles to the centers of the black circles with small dabs of egg white or water. Roll tiny black balls for the eyes and cut very thin black strips for the mouth and attach them to the face with egg white. Attach the finished smiley faces to the cookie with egg white.

SAILBOATS: Each sailboat is made up of two sails (facing in opposite directions), a mast, and a hull. You will need about 8 boats total for each set of pajamas. Start with ½ ounce of white gum paste (about the size of a gumball) and dye about half of it (about the size of a small marble) bright green. Dye a pea-size piece of the gum paste brown.

Roll out the remaining white gum paste to 1⁄16 inch thick on a plastic mat lightly coated with shortening. Cut out 16 sail shapes, approximately ¼ inch by ½ inch for the bigger left side and ¼ inch by 3⁄8 inch for the right side.

Roll the brown gum paste out to 1⁄16 inch and use a paring knife or scalpel to cut skinny strips about ½ inch long for the masts. Finish by rolling the bright green gum paste out to 1⁄16 inch thick and cut out boat shapes, which should be about ¼ inch tall, ¼ inch wide on the bottom, and 5⁄8 inch wide at the top.

Assemble the boats directly on the pajamas using a paintbrush and dabs of egg white. First place the green boats, and then attach the masts, rising from the center of the boat. Next place the larger sail on the left side and the smaller sail on the right. Arrange your boats as if they are sailing in different directions, so they don't bump into each other!

HOT TIP

* Cut some of the motifs in half and place them at the edge of the cookies to give the look of the pattern running off the garment.

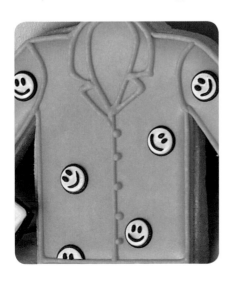

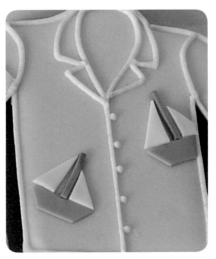

Cookie Templates

PHOTOCOPY THESE TEMPLATES TO HELP WITH YOUR OUTLINES.

STAR COOKIES (PAGE 84)

FARM ANIMAL COOKIES
(PAGE 93)

Cookie Templates
PHOTOCOPY THESE TEMPLATES TO HELP WITH YOUR OUTLINES.

FARM ANIMAL COOKIES
(PAGE 93)

Cookie Templates

PHOTOCOPY THESE TEMPLATES TO HELP WITH YOUR OUTLINES.

HULA KID GINGERBREAD
COOKIES (PAGE 96)

LAMB'S MOUTH

CHICK'S BEAK

BUNNY'S EAR

CHICK'S
HAIR

EASTER COOKIES (PAGE 99)

Cookie Templates

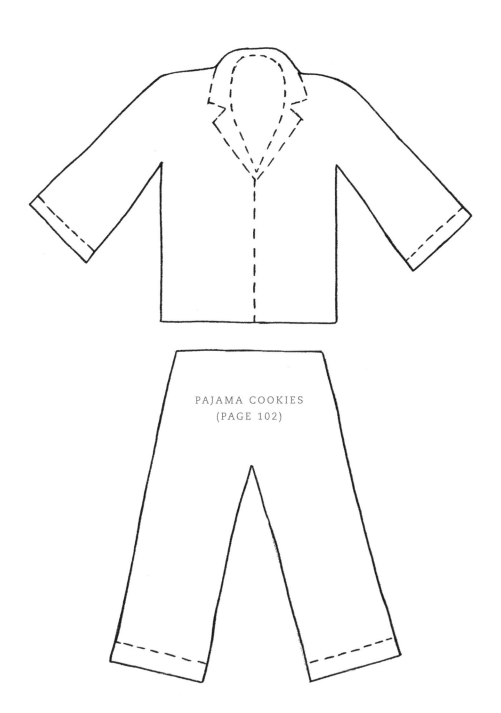

PAJAMA COOKIES
(PAGE 102)

Cupcakes

. . . .

Cupcakes are the perfect confections for kids:
Just watch as their eyes light up
when they see a tray of cupcakes and know they get to
have a delicious little cake topped with
decadent frosting and fun decorations — all to themselves.

You can decorate cupcakes in so many different ways — the possibilities are endless for these versatile treats. Just a simple swirl of frosting or ganache looks fantastic, or you can top that swirl with darling decorations, as with the Garden Mini Cupcakes (page 115). You can also cover a cupcake in fondant for a smooth, sharp look as we do for the Counting Cupcakes (page 118) and the Ornament Cupcakes (page 125). Or you could replicate the look of other foods with our sweet Cupcake Frosting (see the Ice Cream Cupcakes on page 112) or marzipan (like the Burgers and Fries Cupcakes on page 123).

Whatever you do, have fun! And coordinate your cupcake wrappers to enhance the overall design. Chocolate and carrot cupcakes look best in metallic or dark-colored wrappers; pastel or white wrappers work well with a light-colored cake, such as our Yellow Cake (page 65) or Lemon Cake (page 69), that won't show through as much. Be sure that the color of the wrapper goes with the color scheme of your frosting and decorations, too. Present your cupcakes grouped together on a brightly colored background or stacked on tiered plates so the display has height. Finally, be sure to have plenty of cupcakes for all your guests (and maybe a few extras) because no one will want to miss this adorable treat!

Ice Cream Cupcakes

At Confetti Cakes, we get frequent requests for ice cream cakes — but alas, real ice cream would melt before we had a chance to decorate it. These cupcakes, however, will delight any ice cream lover. They are perfect for a birthday party or any summer gathering, and they will keep in the heat! For those who cannot live without an ice cream cake, replace the "scoop" of frosting with real ice cream and keep them in the freezer until you are ready to serve. But remember that those will melt — this version can be on display throughout the entire party. I like to use real cherries as decoration — but I've included instructions here for how to make some out of fondant or gum paste if you so desire.

WHAT YOU NEED

RECIPES

1 cake recipe (see Basic Recipes, pages 64–69)

1½ recipes Cupcake Frosting (page 76)

MATERIALS

Food coloring gels: leaf green, rose pink

EQUIPMENT

Cupcake tins

White party cups (see photo) or cupcake wrappers

Toothpicks

Small offset spatula

Ice cream scoop (#8)

Large bowl filled with hot water (for scooping)

FOR CHERRIES (OPTIONAL)

MATERIALS

1¼ ounces fondant or gum paste

Food coloring gel: super red

Shortening (for rolling fondant or gum paste)

EQUIPMENT

Plastic mat

Ball tool

Tray filled with flour and covered with plastic wrap (for drying the cherries)

TECHNIQUE

Dyeing fondant or gum paste (page 50)

METHOD

One day in advance: *Make the cherries* *(Optional)*

1. Tint all the fondant or gum paste cherry red. On a plastic mat coated with shortening, roll it into a long rope, divide it into 24 sections, and roll each section into a ball.

2. Use the small end of a ball tool to make an indent at the top of each cherry. Make a crease by pulling the ball tool to the side after it makes the indent.

3. Let the cherries rest on a tray or pan filled with flour and covered with plastic wrap. This will allow the cherries to dry and keep the bottoms from becoming flat.

MAKE AND ASSEMBLE THE CUPCAKES

1. Prepare the cake batter as directed. Line the cupcake tins with white party cups. Fill each halfway with batter and bake the cupcakes as directed by the recipe. Let them cool completely.

2. While the cupcakes are cooling, make the frosting. Divide it into three portions and dye one portion pale pink and one portion light green (the color of mint or pistachio ice cream). Reserve the third portion of white frosting for "vanilla" color.

3. Use the #8 size ice cream scoop to "frost" the cupcakes. (You will use more frosting for the scoops than you would for swirls, which is why this project calls for 1½ recipes of frosting.) For best results, keep the frosting cold in the refrigerator. Dip the scoop into a large bowl of hot water and scoop the cold frosting into the center of the cupcakes. Press the edge of the ice cream scoop into the frosting to create the rough edge of ice cream. If you desire an even larger edge, then apply small amounts of frosting directly to the side of the scoop and wrapper and use your hands to shape. Garnish with real or sugar cherries.

HOT TIP

* If you want to create a "sundae bar" using the cupcakes instead of ice cream, set out bowls of cherries, sprinkles, and hot fudge alongside the cupcakes.

Garden Mini Cupcakes

YIELD: 24 mini cupcakes

I love the small size of these adorable cupcakes. They are perfect petit fours if you want to offer just a bit of something sweet or if you're preparing a variety of desserts — or you can make a bunch of them and have an eye-catching display. The mini metallic wrappers we use for these are often used to hold bon bon candies, and they add a touch of shine. The garden theme is perfect for any tea party, flower power bash, or graduation celebration. Here we used Milk Chocolate Ganache as frosting. It has a lighter, sweeter feel than dark chocolate ganache, but still has a rich chocolate taste that kids will adore. But you can use any of our frosting recipes to pipe these cute little treats.

WHAT YOU NEED

RECIPES

¼ recipe Royal Icing (page 78)

½ cake recipe (see Basic Recipes, pages 64–69)

1 recipe Milk Chocolate Ganache (page 77)

MATERIALS

4½ ounces fondant or gum paste

Food-coloring gels: rose pink, coal black, lemon yellow, super red

Shortening (for rolling fondant or gum paste)

Egg whites (optional)

EQUIPMENT

Toothpicks

Small rolling pin

Plastic mat

5-petal flower cutters: ½-inch, ¼-inch

Ball tool (optional)

Pastry bags and plastic couplers

Scissors

Pastry tips: #12, #3, #4, #5, #6

Scalpel or paring knife

Ruler

1 small paintbrush

Mini cupcake tins

Metallic blue wrappers (approximately 1 inch wide and ¾ inch tall)

TECHNIQUES

Dyeing fondant or gum paste (page 50)

Dyeing Royal Icing (page 25)

Filling a pastry bag (page 26)

Piping dots (page 27)

Creating a swirl of frosting (page 33)

METHOD

MAKE THE DECORATIONS

These sugar decorations (the flowers, bumble bees, and ladybugs) do not *need* to be made ahead of time, but they will be easier to handle and place on the cupcakes if they have had time to dry. Plus, it's easier if you allow two days for the cupcakes. Make the sugar decorations on the first day and bake and assemble the cupcakes on the second day.

Here are directions to decorate 24 mini cupcakes with 3 flowers each, bumble bees for 12 cupcakes and ladybugs for 12 cupcakes.

FLOWERS

1. Make the Royal Icing.

2. Dye 1 ounce of fondant or gum paste pale pink. On a plastic mat greased with shortening, roll out the pink dough to approximately ¹⁄₁₆ inch thick.

3. Use the larger 5-petal flower cutter to cut out 24 flowers. Use the smaller cutter to cut out 48 mini flowers. Apply the small end of the ball tool or a small finger to the middle of the flowers to create a little curve.

4. Tint the Royal Icing lemon yellow. Fill a pastry bag fitted with a #3 tip and pipe dots at the centers of the flowers. When ready to assemble, use two mini flowers and one larger flower on each cupcake, as pictured.

BUMBLEBEES

1. Start with 2 ounces of fondant or gum paste. Dye 1 ounce black, ½ ounce bright yellow, and keep ½ ounce white.

2. Divide the black dough into 12 equal pieces. Cut a pea-size amount off each piece and form them into a ball for the heads. Roll the larger pieces into cones about ¾ inch long for the bodies and curl up the pointed ends. Attach the heads to the bodies with dabs of egg white.

3. Roll out the yellow dough as thin as possible on a plastic mat coated with shortening, and cut 3 stripes for each bee (36 stripes total), approximately ⅛ inch wide and 1¼ inches long. Attach the stripes to the bodies with egg whites.

4. Roll the white dough as thin as possible (just like the stripes) and cut 16 teardrop-shaped wings, approximately ⅜ inch wide and ½ inch long. Attach two wings to each bumblebee, just behind the head, with egg whites.

LADYBUGS

1. Dye 1 ounce of fondant or gum paste red and ½ ounce black.

2. Divide the red into 12 equal balls. Roll each ball slightly into an oval shape and cut off a tiny piece on one end to form a flat surface. Use a scalpel or paring knife to make a line down the center of the back to form the wings.

3. Use the black dough to make 12 tiny balls and attach each ball to the flat end of a ladybug body with a brush and some egg whites to form the heads. Roll the remaining black dough (about ¼ ounce) as thin as possible on a plastic mat coated with shortening, and cut out various sizes of dots using #4, #5, and #6 pastry tips. Attach to the backs of the ladybugs with egg whites.

MAKE AND ASSEMBLE THE CUPCAKES

1. Prepare the cake batter as directed. Line the mini cupcake tins with mini wrappers. Fill each halfway with batter, using a pastry bag or a small spoon. Bake the cupcakes as directed by the recipe. Let them cool completely.

2. While the cupcakes are cooling, make the Milk Chocolate Ganache. If you've made the ganache in advance and refrigerated it, bring it back to room temperature for best piping results.

3. Fill a pastry bag fitted with a #12 pastry tip with the Milk Chocolate Ganache. Pipe each cupcake with a mini swirl.

4. Once the cupcakes are frosted, the ganache should set right away. If it is warm where you are working and they are too soft to decorate, place them in the refrigerator for about an hour so the frosting can set before you place the sugar decorations on top. Gently press the decorations into the frosting until they feel secure.

Counting Cupcakes

YIELD: 24 cupcakes

These cupcakes were inspired by a vintage Dr. Seuss poster I saw recently. I love the bright, retro colors — and the use of playful fish to help a little one learn to count! A math lesson is so much fun when it comes with delicious cupcakes and sugar fish. You can customize these cupcakes by focusing on one number (the number 4 for a fourth birthday) or letter (such as an initial) to celebrate a special occasion. If you are short on time but like the idea of the fish, use candy fish instead of making your own. Arrange the cupcakes and fish on a blue platter or tablecloth so the fish can "swim."

WHAT YOU NEED

RECIPES

1 cake recipe (see Basic Recipes, pages 64–69)

½ frosting recipe (see Basic Recipes, pages 71–77)

½ recipe Royal Icing (page 78)

MATERIALS

1¼ pounds fondant to cover cupcakes (plus extra fondant or gum paste for making fish, if desired)

Food-coloring gels: royal blue, lemon yellow, electric green, rose pink, super red, navy blue

Shortening (for rolling fondant)

Egg whites (optional)

EQUIPMENT

Toothpicks

Scalpel or paring knife

Plastic mat

Ruler

Pastry tips: #2, #3, #804

Cupcake tins

Red cupcake wrappers

Small offset spatula

Small rolling pin

Round cookie cutters; 2½-inch, 1⅞-inch

Paring knives

Fondant smoothers

Number cutters, approximately 1 inch tall

Small paintbrush

Pastry bags and plastic couplers

Scissors

TECHNIQUES

Dyeing fondant or gum paste (page 50)

Creating a dome of filling (page 34)

Covering cupcakes with fondant (page 34)

Filling a pastry bag (page 26)

Piping dots (page 27)

METHOD

MAKE THE FISH (*Optional*)

Decide in advance how many fish you want to make. It's fun to make enough fish to coordinate with the numbers on the cupcakes (5 fish for the number 5 cupcake), but you could also make just one fish to go with each cupcake. You can make the fish out of rolled fondant or gum paste. The details will appear finer with gum paste, but it's not necessary to use it. You will need approximately ¼ ounce of fondant or gum paste for **each** fish.

The fish do not *need* to be made ahead of time, but they will be easier to handle if they have had time to dry. If you want to complete these cupcakes in one day, I do suggest making the fish before you start baking and letting them dry for a few hours while you make and assemble the cupcakes. What's most fun about these fish are the colors. I like to use contrasting colors for the fish and the numbers they are connected with.

1. For each fish, dye ¼ ounce of fondant or gum paste the color you desire. On a plastic mat greased with shortening, shape the fondant into a small log, about 1½ inches long and ½ inch wide. Pinch the back of the fish until the middle section is approximately ¼ inch thick.

2. One end of the log will be the head of the fish; flatten the other end to create the tail. Use a paring knife and cut a small V out of the tail end, creating two back fins. Use the dull side of the knife to press lines into the tail.

3. Use a #3 pastry tip to press an eye into the head of the fish face. Use the thin edge of a #804 tip to emboss a mouth into the fish.

4. To create fins, roll out the scraps of fondant as thin as you can and cut out two small triangles, approximately ½ inch long and ³⁄₁₆ inch wide. Round the edges with your fingers and attach the fins, one on each side of the fish, with a dab of egg whites or water.

MAKE AND ASSEMBLE THE CUPCAKES

1. Prepare the cake batter as directed. Line the cupcake tins with red wrappers. Fill each halfway with batter and bake the cupcakes as directed by the recipe. Let them cool completely.

2. While the cupcakes are cooling, make the frosting and Royal Icing. Divide the rolled fondant and dye 6 ounces blue and 2 ounces yellow. Reserve the remaining fondant for the numbers.

3. Create a dome of frosting on each cupcake. On a surface greased with shortening, roll out the blue fondant to ¹⁄₁₆ inch thick. Use the 2½-inch round cookie cutter to cut 24 circles of fondant. Smooth the circles onto the cupcakes. Roll the yellow fondant as thin as possible without tearing it, and cut out 24 smaller circles using the 1⅞-inch round cutter. Center the yellow circles on top of the blue circles. (They should stick on their own, but if not, use a dab of water to hold them.)

4. Once the cupcakes are covered with both circles of fondant, divide the remaining fondant and dye it the colors you want for the numbers. You will need approximately ½ ounce of fondant for each number. Roll the fondant ⅛ inch thick and cut out numbers with the number cutters. Glue the numbers to the centers of the yellow circles using a dab of water.

5. Fill a pastry bag fitted with a #2 tip with white Royal Icing. Use the icing to pipe a ring of dots around the edge of each yellow circle, spaced approximately ⅛ inch apart.

Burgers and Fries Cupcakes

YIELD: 24 cupcakes (12 burgers and 12 fries)

Here's a very sweet interpretation of savory food. Making these reminds me of modeling with Play-Doh, like I did so often when I was little. But we use delicious marzipan instead! A clay gun helps create the details. Kids will have fun assembling these. They might want to dye frosting the color of ketchup — and mustard, too.

WHAT YOU NEED

RECIPES

1 cake recipe (see Basic Recipes, pages 64–69)

½ frosting recipe (see Basic Recipes, pages 71–77)

MATERIALS

8¼ pounds marzipan

Shortening (for sculpting marzipan)

Powdered food coloring: brown, green, yellow, orange, red

Egg whites (optional)

Food coloring gels: buckeye brown, super red, lemon yellow, sunset orange, leaf green

EQUIPMENT

Cupcake tins

Foil cupcake wrappers

Offset spatula

Clay gun with square disc attachment

Medium and small paintbrushes

Toothpicks

Plastic mat

Scalpel or paring knife

Small rolling pin

Round cutters: 1½-inch, 1¼-inch

Ruler

Leaf mold press (optional)

TECHNIQUE

Dyeing marzipan (page 50)

4. Form a hook by gently folding a 1-inch section of rope in half, leaving a loop at the top, and joining the two ends together so they will fit into the hole you made in the base of the hook. Let dry for at least 1 hour.

MAKE AND ASSEMBLE THE CUPCAKES

1. Prepare the cake batter as directed. Line the cupcake tins with gold wrappers. Fill each halfway with batter. Bake the cupcakes as directed by the recipe. Let them cool completely.

2. While the cupcakes are cooling, make the frosting and Royal Icing.

3. Frost the cupcakes with a dome of filling. On a plastic mat greased with shortening, roll out the remaining 12 ounces of fondant to ⅛ inch thick. Use a 2½-inch round cookie cutter to cut 24 circles of fondant. Smooth the circles onto the cupcakes.

4. Once the cupcakes are covered with fondant, use a medium brush to paint the fondant in your desired colors using luster dusts (the specific luster dusts we used for the cupcakes here are detailed below). Create a mixture of luster dust and lemon extract and paint the entire surface of the fondant. Make sure to paint the edges, too!

5. Use a mixture of gold luster dust and lemon extract to paint all the hooks and bases. Let dry for about 20 minutes. Fill a pastry bag fitted with a #1 tip with some Royal Icing. For each cupcake, use the icing to glue a hook into a base. (If the hole is not large enough, use a toothpick to widen it.) Then use the icing to glue the entire base and hook to the top edge of a cupcake.

6. To decorate the cupcakes pictured here (from top to bottom):

SHIMMERY WHITE BACKGROUND: Paint the fondant surface with a mixture of super pearl luster dust and lemon extract. Attach a hook and base. Pipe diagonal lines of white Royal Icing with a #1 pastry tip. Dye a small amount of Royal Icing with red gel and pipe dots in all four corners of intersecting lines with a #2 tip. Let dry for 1 hour. Use a small brush to paint the white lines with gold luster dust and lemon extract. Use another small brush to paint the red dots with a mixture of rouge flambé luster dust and lemon extract.

SHIMMERY DEEP RED BACKGROUND: Paint the fondant surface with rouge flambé luster dust mixed with lemon extract. Attach a hook and base. Have a pair of tweezers and gold dragées on hand. Use a #1 tip to pipe clusters of four dots in white Royal Icing. Use the tweezers to place the dragées directly on top of the piped dots, working quickly to place the dragées before the icing hardens.

SHIMMERY BLUE-GREEN BACKGROUND: Paint the fondant surface with super green luster dust mixed with lemon extract. Attach a hook and base. Use a #1 tip to pipe white Royal Icing in swirls all over the cupcake. Let dry for 1 hour. Use a very small brush to paint the swirls with a mixture of teal luster dust and lemon extract.

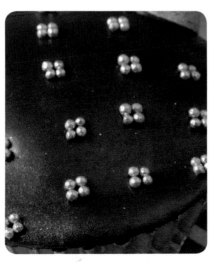

Beach Pail Cupcakes

YIELD: 12 pails

This is the perfect dessert for a beach party, pool party, or any summertime event. If you want to make these in the spring, you could replace the brown sugar with chocolate cookie crumbs and change the color of the pails and — voila! — they're ready for a garden party. Although these are created from cupcakes, they are really little individual cakes — completely decorated and without wrappers.

WHAT YOU NEED

RECIPES

1 cake recipe (see Basic Recipes, pages 64–69)

½ frosting recipe (see Basic Recipes, pages 71–77)

MATERIALS

2 pounds gum paste (for sugar decorations)

Food-coloring gels: royal blue, lemon yellow, sunset orange, leaf green, super red, navy blue, buckeye brown

Shortening (for rolling out fondant and gum paste)

Powdered food coloring: brown

3 pounds fondant

Egg whites (optional)

½ cup brown sugar

EQUIPMENT

Toothpicks

Plastic mat

Small rolling pin

Star cutters: 1-inch, 1½-inch, 2-inch, optional

Small paintbrush

3 x 1-inch leaf cutter or beach ball stripe template (page 131)

Scalpel or paring knife

Template for shovel (page 131)

Pastry tips: #7, #12, #806

Ruler

Cupcake tins

Small serrated knife

Twelve 1¼-inch round cardboards

Pastry bags and plastic couplers

Small offset spatula

Scissors, optional

TECHNIQUES

Dyeing fondant and gum paste (page 50)

Sculpting cake (page 39)

Filling cake (page 38)

Crumb coating cake (page 40)

Creating a dome of filling (page 34)

METHOD

MAKE THE DECORATIONS

Below we give directions for each of the beach decorations (star fish, shovel, and beach ball). Decide how many of each you want to make ahead of time. We have provided directions for one of each pail. These do not *need* to be made ahead of time, but if you want the handle of the shovel to be stiff, you need to give it at least 1 to 2 days to dry on a flat surface lined with parchment paper. We give directions for using gum paste here, but all the decorations can be made with rolled fondant. Using gum paste will result in finer details, but is not necessary. If you plan to complete these cupcakes in one day, make the decorations before you start baking and let them dry for at least a few hours while you assemble the cupcakes.

STARFISH

1. Dye ½ ounce of gum paste the color of sand. Roll it out to ⅛ inch thick on a plastic mat coated with shortening.

2. Cut out 6 stars, 2 with each size of cutter. Use your fingertips, coated with a little shortening, to elongate the "legs" of the stars and to round the ends.

3. Use a toothpick to create texture all over the starfish. Let the starfish dry for at least 1 hour, then dust with brown powdered food coloring using a small brush.

BEACH BALL

1. Form 2 ounces of gum paste into a ball. Then divide another 1¼ ounces into 5 little balls (about ¼ ounce each). Dye each section a different beach ball color: red, orange, navy blue, green, and yellow.

2. Roll out each color as thin as possible and cut out a section of each color with the leaf cutter (or use the template

on page 131). Attach the different colors around the white ball with tiny dabs of egg white or water, lining the edges of each color up with the next and leaving one space for the white to show through. If the colors overlap, use a scalpel to cut away excess.

3. After all colors are applied, use a #806 pastry tip to cut out 2 circles of red gum paste. Attach them to the beach ball on each side where all the colors meet in the center.

SHOVEL

Dye ½ ounce gum paste bright yellow. Roll out to ⅛ inch thick and approximately 3¼ inches long. Use the shovel template (page 131) or draw the shape of a shovel freehand and cut out the shape. Use your fingers to round the edges on the top and bottom of the shovel. Use a #7 pastry tip to cut out a curved hole at the top of the handle. Use a scalpel or paring knife to trim the top corners inside the opening to form the handle. Use the scalpel gently to carve out the scoop of the shovel, leaving a small lip for the shovel and smoothing it out with the back of the scalpel or your finger.

MAKE AND ASSEMBLE THE CUPCAKES

1. Prepare the cake batter as directed. Grease 24 cupcake tins lightly with butter. Fill each halfway with batter and bake the cupcakes as directed by the recipe. Let cool for 20 minutes. Remove from pan, then wrap tightly in plastic wrap and freeze for at least 1 hour. (This makes the cake easier to cut.)

2. While the cupcakes are chilling, make the frosting. Divide the rolled fondant in thirds and dye one portion red, one portion royal blue, and keep the last portion white.

3. For each pail, stack one chilled cupcake on top of another. Use a small serrated knife to create the shape of the pail. To do this, carve small pieces of cake, a little at a time, until the shape of the two-cupcake stack resembles a beach pail, tapering from a wider top to a narrower bottom. The top should be the size you started with and the bottom should be approximately 1¼ inches in diameter.

4. Once you have the shape of the pail, separate the two cupcakes. Attach the bottom cupcake onto a pre-cut 1¼-inch round of cardboard with a dab of frosting. Fill with a thin layer of frosting, about ¼ inch high, and then sandwich them back together. Crumb coat the entire pail. Hold the top of the cupcake as you coat and smooth the sides to keep it from sliding off the bottom cupcake.

5. You will need approximately 4 ounces of fondant, dyed in the color you want, to wrap around each cake. On a surface greased with shortening, roll out the fondant, one color at a time, to ⅛ inch thick. Cut a 9 x 3-inch rectangle, wrap it around the sides of the pail, and join the edges with water. Use a knife or sharp scissors to cut the excess fondant, cutting on an angle that follows the shape of the pail. Trim the top edge so it's ⅛ inch higher than the top of the cake. Save any unused fondant.

6. Using ½ ounce of the fondant left over from covering the pail, roll a strip about 10 inches long, ¼ inch wide and ¼ inch thick. Use your fingers, coated with shortening, to smooth the edges. This will be the top rim of the pail. Moisten the top

edge of the fondant on the pail with water and attach the strip. Make sure the strip is joined in the back of your pail and trim any excess.

7. Make the handles. Use about ½ ounce of gum paste in a contrasting color to the pail and roll it on a plastic mat coated in shortening to ¹⁄₁₆ inch thick. Cut a strip ¹⁄₁₆ inch wide and 5½ inches long. Attach the two ends to the pail rim with dabs of water, letting the handle hang below the rim of the pail. From the same color, cut 2 circles using a #12 pastry tip. Attach the circles to the ends of the handles at the rim of the pail. Cut out two more circles from the original pail color with a #7 tip and stick those to the center of the first circles.

8. Fill the inside of the top of the pail with 3 tablespoons of frosting and spoon approximately 2 teaspoons of brown sugar "sand" inside the pail. Place the sugar decorations in before the sand has time to harden.

DECORATE THE PAILS

POLKA DOTS

Roll out ¼ ounce of gum paste paper-thin on a plastic mat coated with shortening. Use a #12 tip to cut out dots and then attach them directly to the pail with tiny dabs of water applied with a brush.

STRIPES

Roll out about ¼ ounce of three different colors of gum paste paper-thin. Cut stripes about 10 inches long and in varying widths (here we used ½ inch of red, ¼ inch of blue, and ¹⁄₁₆ inch of orange). Attach the stripes to the pails with water.

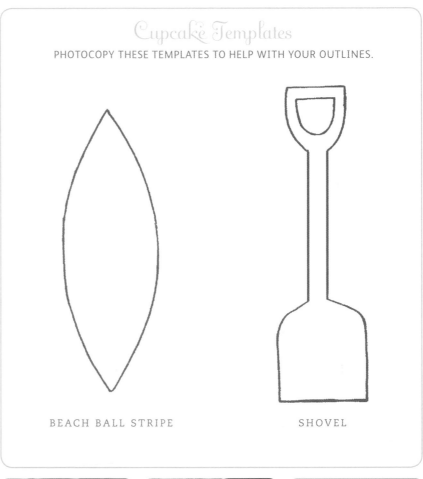

Cupcake Templates

PHOTOCOPY THESE TEMPLATES TO HELP WITH YOUR OUTLINES.

BEACH BALL STRIPE   SHOVEL

Mini Cakes

Every mini cake is a work of art unto itself, guaranteed to make whoever gets it feel like a star.
Kids will always remember a mini cake made just for them in the shape of something they love.
Mini cakes generally feed one to three people each. Their small size means that they are fun to create in the form of little objects like conversation hearts (page 138) or MP3 players (page 151).
The ideas for many mini cakes can be translated to larger cakes if you want to serve a crowd.

Though making a mini cake is generally less time consuming than making a large, complicated sculpted cake, remember that the individual cakes do tend to require much attention to detail and effort — and you'll have to repeat that effort for each mini cake you make! Therefore we suggest mini cakes for small parties — such as a child's birthday party with just a few friends — and as beautiful, personal gifts, but not for big events with dozens of people.

Mini cakes are wonderful vehicles for practicing your sculpting skills on a less intimidating scale. The Conversation Heart Mini Cakes (page 138), Pumpkin Mini Cakes (page 147), and MP3 Mini Cakes (page 151) all require some sculpting, but are straightforward enough for beginners to try. For sculpted mini cakes, be sure to use a sturdy filling such as Milk Chocolate Ganache (page 77) or a variation of buttercream. The Slice of Cake Brownie Mini Cakes (page 135) and Spring Mini Cakes (page 143) are great places to practice filling layers of cake and covering cakes with fondant.

The projects in this chapter can generally be completed in a day, though some of the decorations are best made a day or more in advance. Still, they are time-consuming and you need to plan ahead and give yourself ample opportunity to complete them without getting stressed out. Another bonus to mini cakes? They are small enough that they tend not to require doweling, and you won't need to worry about their internal structure the way you do with some large cakes.

Slice of Cake Brownie Mini Cakes

YIELD: 5 individual cakes

Everyone loves a slice of cake... so why not a slice of cake that's actually layers of brownie? These mini cakes are extra special because they are made from Confetti Cakes' amazing brownies. Our brownies have become famous because they are so delicious — and because we don't sell them. We only give them out on very special occasions. People have been requesting the recipe for years. So we included it in this book, and here we show you how to sculpt it into a work of art! This is a fun way to celebrate any occasion. Mix and match the colors of frosting for a beautiful display.

WHAT YOU NEED

RECIPES

1 recipe Amazing Chocolate Brownies (page 63)

1 frosting recipe (see Basic Recipes, pages 71–77)

MATERIALS

1⅛ pounds fondant (store-bought or page 80)

1 ounce gum paste (optional, for candles)

Food-coloring gels: royal blue, violet, lemon yellow, leaf green, avocado green, rose pink, sunset orange

Shortening (for rolling fondant and gum paste)

Egg whites (optional)

EQUIPMENT

Clay gun with ³⁄₁₆-inch circle disc (optional)

Toothpicks

Small paintbrush

Brownie wedge templates (page 154)

Cardboard or foam core

X-acto knife

Scissors

Serrated knife

Small offset spatula

Ruler

Plastic mat

Small rolling pin

Scalpel or paring knife

Pastry tip #809 (or ⅝-inch circle cutter)

Small dowel (optional)

TECHNIQUES

Dyeing fondant and gum paste (page 50)

Dyeing Royal Icing and buttercream (page 25)

Making a template (page 31)

Filling cake (page 38)

Crumb coating cake (page 40)

METHOD

At least one day in advance: *Make the candles (Optional)*

You can make the candles from fondant if you have a few days to let them dry so they harden and stand straight. If you need them to dry more quickly, use gum paste. The quantities described below will make 5 candles, but it's a good idea to make extra in case of breakage. The measurements are the same for both fondant and gum paste.

1. Dye ½ ounce of fondant or gum paste bright orange and ¼ ounce bright yellow. If you have a clay gun, press the orange dough through a ³⁄₁₆-inch round disc and cut it into five separate 3-inch pieces. If you don't have a clay gun, roll the dough (on a smooth surface greased with shortening) into five 3-inch logs, about ³⁄₁₆ inch thick. Bring one end of each log to a point and allow them to dry, at least overnight, before attaching the flame.

2. Divide the yellow gum paste into 5 equal pieces. Roll each piece into a ball and form into a teardrop shape to resemble a flame. Poke a hole in the bottom of the flame with a toothpick and stick the point of the candle into the hole, attaching it with some egg whites (or water).

3. For the candle stripes, roll out ¼ ounce of white gum paste as thin as you can on a smooth surface greased with shortening. Cut 15 strips that are ¹⁄₁₆ inch wide and 5 inches long. Brush the backs of the strips with a little dabs of egg white (or water). Attach the strips to the hardened candles, coiling three strips around each candle, evenly spaced.

MAKE AND ASSEMBLE THE MINI CAKES

1. Prepare the brownie batter and bake in a half-sheet pan as directed in the recipe. Let cool for 20 minutes. Remove from pan, wrap tightly in plastic wrap, and freeze for at least 1 hour. (This will make the brownies easier to cut.)

2. While the brownies are chilling, make the filling. Dye the filling in your desired colors.

3. Cut the brownies, using the wedge-shaped template (page 154), into 15 wedges, 2¾ inches wide and 4 inches long. For each mini cake, you will use three wedges of brownie.

4. For each cake, place the first wedge on a plate or flat surface. Coat the top with approximately ½ inch of filling and place the next wedge on top, then repeat. Each mini cake will consist of 3 layers of brownie and 2 layers of filling. After the top layer of brownie is on, push down slightly to secure the layers. Place the cakes in the refrigerator and chill for 1 hour or until the frosting is firm.

5. Crumb coat the top and backside of the brownie wedges with a very thin layer of frosting. Use a serrated knife to trim any excess frosting from the sides and top of each slice.

6. Dye the fondant (approximately 3 ounces per mini cake) your desired colors. For the slices pictured here, we used pale purple, lime green, and white.

7. On a plastic mat greased with shortening, roll out the fondant to ⅛ inch thick and use the template for the fondant (page 154) to cut the fondant into 5 pieces. Cover only the top and the backside of each cake and trim with a scalpel or paring knife.

8. To add polka dots, use ½ ounce of fondant per mini cake and dye it the desired color. Here we used yellow, pale blue, and pale pink. Roll out the fondant as thin as possible and use a #809 pastry tip to cut out about 8 polka dots for each mini cake. Use a small paintbrush to attach the dots with little dabs of egg whites or water.

9. Use a small dowel or toothpick to create a hole in the center of each wedge and insert a dried candle into the hole.

HOT TIPS

* If you don't have any fondant to cover the slices, use frosting on the outsides of the brownie wedges to decorate.

* You can use this method to make these mini cakes out of actual cake, but don't let them sit out uncovered — keep them wrapped in plastic wrap or they will dry out and become stale.

* If you don't have time to make sugar candles, use real birthday candles; they look cute, too!

Conversation Heart Mini Cakes

YIELD: 6 individual cakes

Inspired by those playful candy hearts that are everywhere on Valentine's Day, these cakes are a perfect way to let someone know you care, on Valentine's Day or anytime. Make a set of them for a party or just make one special cake for someone you love. Change the words to suit the recipient! Think about personalizing it with a name or a unique message.

WHAT YOU NEED

RECIPES

1 cake recipe, any flavor (see Basic Recipes, pages 64–69)

1 frosting recipe (see Basic Recipes, pages 71–77)

MATERIALS

2¼ pounds fondant

Food-coloring gels: rose pink, lemon yellow, leaf green, violet, electric pink

Cornstarch (for rolling fondant)

½ ounce gum paste (for letters)

Shortening (for rolling gum paste)

Egg whites (optional)

EQUIPMENT

4¼ x 4¼-inch heart cutter, or template (page 155)

X-acto knife

Six 4¼ x 4¼-inch pieces heart-shaped cardboard or foam core hearts

Small offset spatula

Small serrated knife

Toothpicks

Large rolling pin

Strainer

Dry pastry brush

Scalpel or paring knife

Fondant smoothers

Plastic mat

Small rolling pin

Letter cutters, approximately ⅝ x ½-inch (optional)

Small paintbrush

TECHNIQUES

Making a template (page 31)

Filling cake (page 38)

Crumb coating cake (page 40)

Dyeing fondant and gum paste (page 50)

Covering cake with fondant (page 41)

METHOD

1. Prepare the cake batter and bake in a half-sheet pan as directed in the recipe. Let cool for 20 minutes, remove from pan, then wrap tightly in plastic wrap and freeze for at least 1 hour. (This makes the cake easier to cut.)

2. While the cake is chilling, make the frosting.

3. Cut the cake, using the heart cutter or template, into 12 hearts.

4. Each mini cake will consist of 2 layers of cake and 1 layer of filling. For each cake, place a dab of filling on each cardboard heart and then place one cake heart on top. With an offset spatula, coat the bottom layer with approximately ½ inch of filling and place another heart on top of that. After the top layer of cake is on, push down slightly to secure the layers. Place the hearts in the refrigerator and chill for 1 hour or until the frosting is firm.

5. Use a small serrated knife to trim the cakes into the shape of a rounded heart, approximately 2½ inches high. Round the point of the heart as well as the top and bottom edges for a softer look. Cut away any excess cardboard with a serrated knife or scissors. Crumb coat each cake with a thin layer of frosting.

6. Divide the fondant into 6-ounce sections (you'll need that much to cover each cake) and dye each section your desired color. For the hearts pictured here, we used pale purple, pale pink, lime green, pale yellow, and white.

7. On a smooth surface dusted with cornstarch, roll out the fondant to ⅛ inch thick. Cover each cake with rolled fondant and trim any excess fondant.

8. To make the letters, dye approximately ½ ounce of gum paste hot pink. On a plastic mat greased with shortening, roll out the gum paste paper thin (about 1⁄32 inch) and cut out the letters using cutters. Trim the letters so they're straight. Though it's not necessary, it is easiest if you let the letters dry for a few hours so they have time to harden before placing them on the cakes. Once they are firm to the touch you can arrange them on the cakes to determine the best placement before gluing. Attach the letters to the tops of the cakes with a dab of egg whites or water.

HOT TIP

* If you don't have letter cutters or you're short on time, pipe the message with Royal Icing or write it using edible food markers.

Spring Mini Cakes

YIELD: 5 mini cakes (15 to 20 servings)

I love the fun and whimsical feel of these cakes — each looks like an individually wrapped present. We have made large tiered cakes designed in these patterns, but I think the individual cakes are unexpected and elegant and make for a beautiful assortment for a birthday, Easter, or any springtime party.

WHAT YOU NEED

RECIPES

2 cake recipes (see Basic Recipes, pages 64–69)

1 frosting recipe (see Basic Recipes, pages 71–77)

½ recipe Royal Icing (page 78)

MATERIALS

15 ounces gum paste

Food-coloring gels: ribbon pink, rose pink, super red, leaf green, lemon yellow

Shortening (for rolling gum paste)

Egg whites (optional)

4 pounds fondant

Cornstarch (for rolling fondant)

EQUIPMENT

Toothpicks

Plastic mats

Small and large rolling pins

Ruler

Scalpel or paring knife

Paper towels

Small paintbrush

Daisy cutter, approximately 1 inch wide

Ball tool

Shallow egg carton (optional)

Leaf cutter, approximately 1½ inches long and ½ inch wide (optional)

Letter cutters, approximately 1½ inches high (optional)

Five 4 x 4-inch cardboard or foam core squares

Small offset spatula

Small serrated knife

Strainer

Dry pastry brush

Fondant smoothers

Pastry bag and coupler

Pastry tips: #2, #10, #806, #809

TECHNIQUES

Dyeing fondant and gum paste (page 50)

Filling cake (page 38)

Crumb coating cake (page 40)

Covering cake with fondant (page 41)

Piping dots (page 27)

METHOD

Two days to one week in advance: *Make the bow (see illustrations on page 145).*

1. Dye approximately 4 ounces of gum paste your desired color. Here we chose hot pink. On a plastic mat greased with shortening, roll it out into a sheet approximately ¹⁄₁₆ inch thick. Cut out a 2 x 11-inch strip. Cut a paper towel in half and twist it into two logs (about 3 inches long).

2. Place the paper towel logs directly on top of the 2 x 11-inch gum paste strip, and bring the ends of the strip together, over the paper towels, in the center, forming two loops. (Draping the loops over the paper towels keeps them from collapsing.) Attach the ends to the middle using a drop of water or egg whites. Pinch the center to create the look of a real ribbon tied into a bow.

3. From the same sheet of gum paste cut out another small strip approximately ¾ inch wide and long enough to wrap around the center of the ribbon, about 3 inches. Wrap it around the center of the bow and attach the ends on the bottom with water or egg whites.

4. To make the ribbon tails, cut one 8 x ¾-inch strip of gum paste and cut that strip in half. Cut out a triangle from the bottom of each tail. Let the

tails dry on top of a box, allowing them to lie just as a real ribbon would over a box, making sure that the ends that will sit under the bow are flat.

Two days to one week in advance: *Make the daisies and leaves.*

DAISIES

Roll out 1 ounce of white gum paste as thin as you can on a plastic mat coated with shortening. Use the daisy cutter to cut out about 15 flowers. Place one flower at a time in the center of your hand. Use the ball tool to thin the individual petals of the daisy, then lightly pinch the ends. Let the flowers dry with their petals raised, either in a shallow egg carton or on the sides of a sheet tray.

LEAVES

Dye 1 ounce of gum paste lime green and roll it out to 1/16 inch thick on a plastic mat coated with shortening. Cut out approximately 30 leaves, either using a leaf cutter or a paring knife. Use your fingers to curve the edges of each leaf slightly, then let them dry on the edge of a sheet tray so they take on a curved shape.

MAKE AND ASSEMBLE THE MINI CAKES

1. Prepare the cake batter and bake in two half-sheet pans as directed in the recipe. Let them cool for 20 minutes, remove from pans, then wrap tightly in plastic wrap and freeze for at least one hour. (This will make the cakes easier to cut.)

2. While the cakes are chilling, make the frosting and Royal Icing.

3. Cut the cake into fifteen 4 x 4-inch squares. For each cake, place a dab of frosting on each cardboard square and place a square of cake on top.

4. Coat the bottom layer of cake with approximately 1/2 inch of filling and place the next layer of cake on top, then repeat. Each cake will consist of 3 layers of cake and 2 layers of filling. After the top layer of cake is on, push down slightly to secure the layers. They should be approximately 4-inch cubes. Place the cubes in the refrigerator and chill for 1 hour or until the frosting is firm.

5. Make sure the edges are completely even by trimming with a serrated knife. Cut away any cardboard that is showing either with a serrated knife or scissors. Crumb coat each cake with a thin layer of frosting.

6. Dye the fondant your desired colors. For the cakes pictured here, we used pale green, pale pink, hot pink, lime green, and white. You will use approximately 12 ounces of fondant to cover each cake.

7. On a smooth surface dusted with cornstarch, roll out the fondant to 1/8 inch thick. Cover each cake with rolled fondant and trim. Use the fondant smoothers and your fingertips to create straight sides and sharp corners.

8. To decorate the individual cakes as pictured here, follow the specific instructions below. If you want to add letters, dye approximately 3 ounces of gum paste hot pink. On a plastic mat greased with shortening, roll out the gum paste to 1/4 inch thick. Cut out the letters with your letter cutters and trim them so they are straight. Decorate the letters using white Royal Icing in a pastry bag fitted with a #2 tip. Pipe dots in a random pattern.

DAISY CAKE

This cake is covered in pale pink fondant, created using the rose pink gel color. Fill a pastry bag fitted with a #2 pastry tip with white Royal Icing. Use the icing to attach three sets of two leaves to each side of the cake. Attach one daisy with each set of leaves as shown. Dye 1/4 ounce of gum paste bright pink, roll it out to 1/16 inch thick, and cut out 15 circles using a #10 pastry tip. Attach the circles to the centers of the daisies with a dab of egg whites or water. Pipe three dots of white Royal Icing with a #2 tip on each side of the cake to fill the spaces between the flowers.

PALE GREEN DOT CAKE

This cake is covered in pale green fondant, created using a small amount of leaf green gel color and a touch of lemon yellow. Fill a small pastry bag fitted with a #2 tip with hot pink Royal Icing. Pipe hot pink dots in nine horizontal rows on each side. Every other row should line up, and the rows in between should have the dots fall in the center of the rows above and below. Pipe in a consecutive pattern, and use a ruler to guide you by placing it at the bottom of the cake.

HOT PINK POLKA DOT CAKE

This cake is covered with hot pink fondant that was made from ribbon pink and super red food-coloring gels. Dye 1 ounce of gum paste lime green and roll it out to 1/16 inch thick. Cut four strips that are 3/8 inch wide and 4 inches long for the bottom border of the cake. Attach them to the bottom edge of the cake with a dab of water or egg whites. Use a #809 pastry tip to cut out about 15 dots and place them on the cake with dabs of water and a small paintbrush. Use a pastry bag fitted with a #2 pastry tip and filled with white Royal Icing to pipe borders around each dot and evenly space along the bottom border.

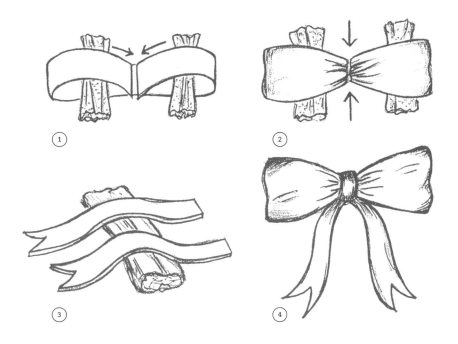

PLAID CAKE

This cake is covered in white fondant. Divide 3 ounces of gum paste in half and dye one portion hot pink and the other portion green. Roll out the two colors, in separate sheets, to 1/16 inch thick on plastic mats coated with shortening. Use a ruler and a paring knife to cut different size stripes in order to create a random pattern. We cut all the horizontal stripes first and placed them on the sides of the cake and then finished with longer stripes that intersected at the top. Attach the stripes by brushing the backs with a tiny amount of water.

From top to bottom, these are the sizes we used horizontally on four sides, leaving the top blank:

> Green: 1/2-inch
>
> Green: 1/4-inch
>
> Green: 1/8-inch
>
> Pink: 3/8-inch
>
> Pink: 1/4-inch
>
> Pink: 3/4-inch

From left to right, these are the sizes we used vertically — they intersect on top:

> Green: 1/4-inch
>
> Pink: 3/4-inch
>
> Green: 1/2-inch
>
> Pink: 1/8-inch
>
> Pink: 1/4-inch

BOW CAKE

This cake is covered in lime green fondant, made from leaf green and lemon yellow food coloring gels. Dye 1 ounce of gum paste hot pink and roll it out to 1/16 inch thick. Use a #806 pastry tip to cut out approximately 64 dots. Glue them onto the sides of the cake with little dabs of water applied with a small paintbrush. Using a small paintbrush, attach the two ribbon tails to the cake with Royal Icing, then attach the bow on top of the two tails with the same icing. Hide the place where they are connected, only applying icing under the two larger parts of the bow and not in the center, so the bow looks like it was tied with one piece of ribbon.

Pumpkin Mini Cakes

YIELD: 3 pumpkins (about 9 servings)

Although these cakes are shaped like little pumpkins, their funny faces remind me of the Mr. Potato Head toy. Even without the faces they are perfect for a Halloween party — but if you decorate them with eyes, noses, and mouths, the kids are sure to crack up. It's also fun to make these cakes and have kids help you decorate them with edible food markers or sugar dough.

WHAT YOU NEED

RECIPES

1 cake recipe (see Basic Recipes, pages 64–69)

1 frosting recipe (see Basic Recipes, pages 71–77)

MATERIALS

1⅛ pounds fondant

Food coloring gels: sunset orange, super red, leaf green, buckeye brown, lemon yellow, coal black, rose pink, violet, royal blue

Cornstarch (for rolling fondant)

7 ounces gum paste (for stems and decorations)

Egg whites (optional)

Shortening (for rolling gum paste)

EQUIPMENT

4-inch round cutter

Three 4-inch round cardboard or foam core pieces

Small offset spatula

Small serrated knife

Toothpicks

Large and small rolling pins

Strainer

Ruler

Dry pastry brush

Paring knife

Fondant smoothers

Scalpel

Plastic mat

Small paintbrush

Pastry tips: #7, #10, #12, #804, #806, #808

TECHNIQUES

Filling cake (page 38)

Crumb coating cake (page 40)

Sculpting cakes (page 39)

Dyeing fondant and gum paste (page 50)

Covering cake with fondant (page 41)

METHOD

MAKE AND ASSEMBLE THE MINI CAKES

1. Prepare the cake batter and bake in a half-sheet pan as directed in the recipe. Let it cool for 20 minutes, remove from pan, then wrap tightly in plastic wrap and freeze for at least one hour. (This will make the cake easier to cut.)

2. While the cake is chilling, make the frosting.

3. Cut the cake into nine 4-inch rounds. For each cake, place a dab of frosting on each cardboard round, and place a round of cake on top of that.

4. Each cake will consist of 3 layers of cake and 2 layers of filling. Coat the bottom layer with approximately ½ inch of filling and place the next layer of cake on top and repeat. After the top layer of cake is on, push down slightly to secure the layers. Each cake should be about 4 inches high. Place the cakes in the refrigerator and chill for 1 hour or until the frosting is firm.

5. Once the cakes are firm to the touch, sculpt the shape of the pumpkins. For each cake, use a small serrated knife to round the edges and form the cake into a squashed looking ball. Once you have the general shape, carve six V-shaped grooves into the sides of the cake. Carve the center of the top of the cake away slightly to form a dimple for the stem. Trim with a serrated knife or scissors so it doesn't show. Crumb coat each cake with a thin layer of frosting.

6. Dye the fondant pumpkin orange by mixing orange and a tiny bit of brown gel. You will use approximately 6 ounces of orange fondant to cover each cake.

7. On a smooth surface dusted with cornstarch, roll out the fondant to ⅛ inch thick. Cover each cake with rolled fondant and trim, making sure the fondant reaches all the way to the edge of the cardboard under the pumpkin. Use the fondant smoothers and your fingertips to shape the fondant into the grooves on the sides of the cakes.

8. Form the stems for each cake. Have fun and make each one look a little different! Dye 4 ounces of gum paste moss green and divide into three separate pieces. Roll each piece into a ball and then form the ball into the shape of a fried egg, round and thicker in the center than at the edges. To do this, use a small rolling pin to thin out the edges of the ball on all sides, leaving a ½-inch bump in the center of the circle. The bottom should be 1¼ inches wide. Pull the extra gum paste in the center of the circle upwards to form a stem and cut it at 1½ inches tall. (If you don't have gum paste you can make the stems out of fondant, though they may take a little longer to dry.)

9. Form the shape of the bottom of the stem by cutting away five triangular pieces to create the six triangular sections at the bottom of the stem. Pinch each triangle into a point.

10. Use the back end of a scalpel or the back of a paring knife to create the lines of the stem. Line up each triangle with a groove on the top of the pumpkin. Curve the stem and pinch the edges to make them sharp. Gently press the end of the stem to create a little indent. Attach the stem on top of the cake, in the center, with water or egg whites.

DECORATE THE CAKES

At this point I think the little pumpkin cakes look great, all on their own. But if you would like to create the faces on the cakes, follow these instructions.

NERVOUS FACE

1. Divide about 1 ounce of gum paste into four ¼-ounce sections and dye one yellow, one black, and one lime green. Leave one white.

2. Roll out the yellow gum paste about ⅛ inch thick on a plastic mat coated with shortening. Cut two eyes with a #808 pastry tip. Round the edges with your fingers.

3. Roll out the white gum paste very thin and cut out two circles with a #804 pastry tip. Roll out the black gum paste very thin and cut out two tiny back circles with a #7 pastry tip.

4. To form the eyes, attach the yellow circle to the pumpkin with a dab of egg white or water. Attach the white circle to the yellow, then the black to the white.

5. Form the nose with a pea-size ball of lime green gum paste and attach it to the pumpkin, between the eyes, with water or egg whites.

6. Roll the black gum paste as thin as you can and cut tiny strips for the two eyebrows and the mouth. To attach the mouth, brush a small amount of water on the cake where you want the mouth to be and place the black strip across that space. Use a toothpick to push the mouth up and down to form a wavy line. Attach the eyebrows with water or egg whites.

GIRLY FACE

1. Dye ½ ounce of gum paste red, ¼ ounce pink, ¼ ounce lavender, ¼ ounce black, and a pinch light blue.

2. Use your hands to form the red gum paste into 2 lips (top and bottom).

3. Roll out half of the pink gum paste paper thin and cut it into the shape of a dome no bigger than the lips, flat on one side and curved on the other. Attach it to the pumpkin where you want the lips to go, flat edge facing up. Attach the lips over the pink gum paste, with a bit of pink showing between the lips, using some water or egg whites.

4. Form the nose with a tiny ball of pink gum paste and attach it to the pumpkin above the lips with water or egg whites.

5. Roll out the white gum paste to ½ inch thick and cut out two eyes with a

#806 pastry tip. Shape them slightly into ovals. Roll out the light blue paste as thin as possible and cut out two circles with a #12 pastry tip, then roll out the black gum paste and cut out two tiny circles with a #7 pastry tip.

6. Attach the white circles, then the light blue, then the black to form the eyes. Roll out the lavender gum paste as thin as possible and cut a circle using a #808 pastry tip. Cut the circle in half and pinch the ends, then place the half circles over the tops of the eyes to create eyelids.

7. Cut tiny strips from the rolled out black gum paste to form the edges of the eyelids and the eyelashes. First attach black lines to the bottom of the eyelashes, then cut various sizes of eyelashes and glue them on with little dabs of water or egg whites. Be careful not to use too much moisture or the black dye may bleed.

SILLY FACE

1. Divide 1 ounce of gum paste into four sections and dye one light blue, one black, and one red. Keep one section white.

2. Roll out the white gum paste to ¼ inch thick and cut two circles with a #808 pastry tip. Shape them slightly to form into ovals. Roll out the light

blue gum paste to ⅛ inch thick and cut out two circles with a #804 pastry tip. Roll out the black gum paste very thin and cut two circles with a #10 pastry tip.

3. Attach the white ovals to the pumpkin, then attach the light blue circles at the bottom, on the side closest to the other eye. Repeat with the black circles on top of the light blue circles to form the eyes.

4. Cut tiny strips from the rolled out black gum paste for the eyebrows and the mouth. To attach the mouth, brush a small amount of water on the cake in the area where you want the mouth to be and place the black strip across that space. Use a toothpick to push the mouth up and down to form a wavy line. Attach the eyebrows.

5. Form the tongue by rolling the red gum paste out to ⅛ inch and forming a ¾ x ⅜-inch rectangle. Make a seam down the middle with the back of the scalpel or paring knife and attach one end to the pumpkin with some water or egg whites. Make sure the end you attach is flat against the pumpkin's face and placed just above the mouth. Curve the tongue slightly with your fingers.

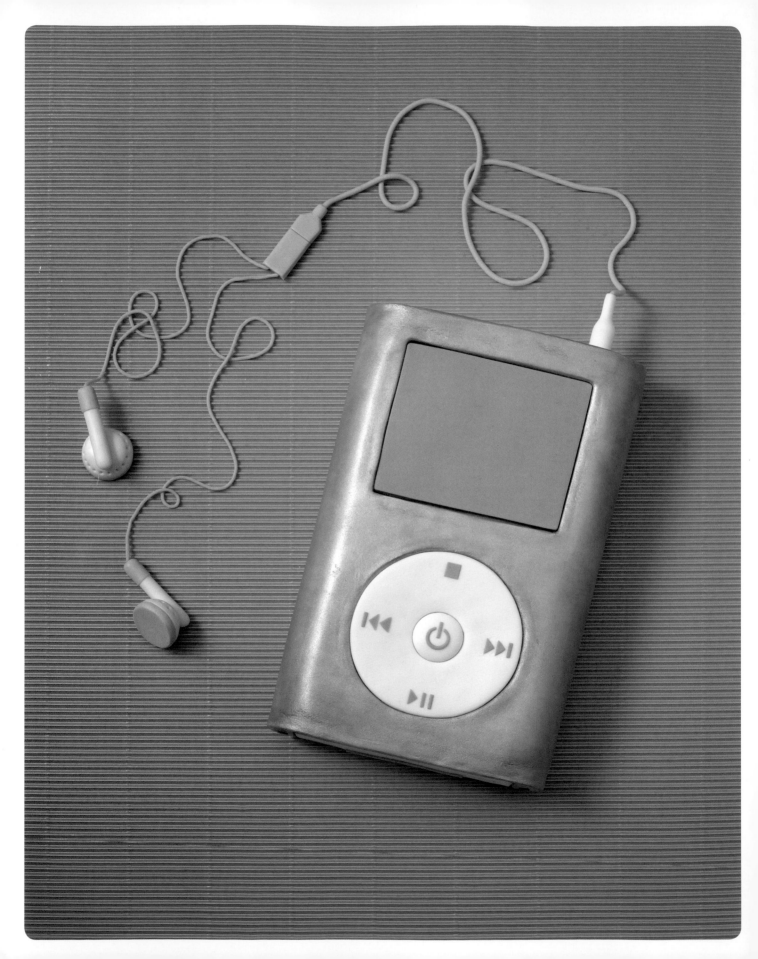

MP3 Mini Cakes

YIELD: Two 8 x 4-inch MP3 players (14 to 16 servings)

MP3 players are fun to customize for the kid in your life who treasures his or her player and loves listening to playlists of favorite songs. Make the cake to match the real player's color, and personalize it further by writing something special in the middle of the screen. You can divide the recipe in half if you want just one mini cake, but it looks great if you make two and place them on a diagonal to each other.

WHAT YOU NEED

RECIPES

1 cake recipe (see Basic Recipes, pages 64–69)

½ frosting recipe (see Basic Recipes, pages 71–77)

MATERIALS

2 pounds fondant

Cornstarch (for rolling out fondant)

Food-coloring dusts: blue petal, pearl luster, metallic silver

Lemon extract

1¼ pounds gum paste

Food-coloring gels: coal black, buckeye brown

Shortening (for rolling out gum paste)

Egg whites (optional)

EQUIPMENT

X-acto knife

Ruler

Small serrated knife

Two 8 x 4-inch rectangular cardboard or foam core pieces

Small offset spatula

Edible marker (optional)

Round cutters: ⅞ inch, 1 inch, 3⅛ inch

Large and small rolling pins

Strainer

Dry pastry brush

Scalpel or paring knife

Fondant smoothers

Veining tool

Pastry tips: #12, #804

Toothpicks

Small and large paintbrushes

Plastic mat

Clay gun with ¹⁄₁₆-inch and ¹⁄₃₂-inch round disc attachments (optional)

TECHNIQUES

Filling cake (page 38)

Crumb coating cake (page 40)

Covering cake with fondant (page 41)

Painting with powders and dusts (page 50)

Dyeing gum paste (page 50)

METHOD

1. Prepare the cake batter and bake in a half-sheet pan as directed in the recipe. Let it cool for 20 minutes, remove from pan, then wrap tightly in plastic wrap and freeze for at least one hour. (This will make the cake easier to cut.)

2. While the cake is chilling, make the frosting.

3. Cut the cake, using a ruler and serrated knife, into four 8 x 5-inch rectangles.

4. For each cake, place a dab of filling on each piece of cardboard and place one rectangle of cake on top. The cakes' edges will overhang the sides of the cardboard until you carve. Coat the bottom layer with approximately ½ inch of filling and place another rectangle on top. Each cake will consist of 2 layers of cake and 1 layer of filling. After the top layer of cake is on, push down slightly to secure the layers. The cakes should be approximately 2 inches high. Place the cakes in the refrigerator and chill for 1 hour or until the frosting is firm.

5. Use a serrated knife to trim the cakes and to give the MP3 player its general shape and details. Create rounded edges on the long sides of the player

by carving about ¾ inch off the top **and** bottom of both sides Trim more cake away, a little at a time, to finish the rounded edge. The sides of the cakes should be completely rounded while the top and bottom ends should be completely flat with curved sides. **Refer to the photo or a real MP3 player to assist your carving.** Cut away any cardboard that is showing either with a serrated knife or scissors.

6. For the screen, start ½ inch in from the top edge of the cake and measure a rectangle that is 3⅝ inches wide and 3 inches high. You can mark this off with an edible marker or lightly score the cake with a paring knife and a ruler. Carefully cut straight lines ¼ inch deep on all the edges, leaving the corners slightly rounded, and remove the cake within that rectangle. If you cut too much cake don't worry — you can always fill in afterwards.

7. For the control button, use a 3¼-inch round cutter to mark the area and carve ¼ inch deep into the cake and remove the cake within the circle. The circle should be centered amidst the screen, the bottom edge, and the sides of the cake. If you want to add extra detail to the cake, carve a 2 x ¾ x ¼-inch deep USB connector into the center of the bottom edge of the cake.

8. Crumb coat each cake with a thin layer of frosting. Be extra careful around the screen, button and connector areas so you do not lose any definition. If the cake is difficult to frost around the detail areas, refrigerate or freeze it until it is firm.

9. To cover each cake, use approximately 1 pound of white fondant rolled out

to ⅛ inch thick. Once the entire cake is covered and the edges are trimmed, use your finger or a veining tool to indent the fondant against the screen, control button, and connector areas. Make sure the fondant is flush against the cake.

10. Use the back of a scalpel to emboss rectangles 4 inches wide and 1¾ inches tall on the top and bottom ends of the player. These rectangles should have curved edges, and they will not be painted. As pictured, create small holes on either side of the rectangle (using a toothpick).

11. For a metallic blue cake, paint the entire cake, except for the two rectangles you just embossed, with a mixture of pearl luster dust, blue petal dust, and lemon extract. (You can paint this cake any color you wish. I would like one the same color as my own pink MP3 player!)

12. To add the screen on top of the fondant, dye approximately 4 ounces of gum paste medium gray. On a plastic mat greased with shortening, roll out the

gum paste to ¼ inch thick and cut a rectangle about 3½ inches wide and 2⅞ inches long. The size will vary based on the screen you carved out earlier on the cake. Cut the screen to fit. Before placing the gray gum paste rectangle into the screen area, use your paring knife to add a curved shape to the corners. Attach the screen to the cake with a dab of water. Reserve any leftover gray gum paste.

13. For the control button, roll 2 ounces of white gum paste on a plastic mat greased with shortening out to ¼ inch thick. Use the round cutters to cut out one 3⅛-inch circle (this will be the outer circle) and, from the middle of that circle, one ⅞-inch circle (this will be the control button). Save the control button circle to use later. Use your fingers to taper the edges of the cut-out in the larger outer circle, then **re-cut** the hole with the ⅞-inch round cutter. Place outer circle into the circle on the cake, then insert the control button circle into the center of the outer circle.

14. Use the left over gray gum paste from the screen to create details on the control buttons and around the USB connector. Roll the gray gum paste paper-thin (approximately ¹⁄₃₂ inch thick) and cut out the proper symbols for each button. Refer to the photo as you go.

One square: ¼ x ¼-inch

Five triangles: ¼ x ³⁄₁₆-inch

Four lines: ⅛ x ¼-inch

One line: ⅛ x ⁵⁄₁₆-inch for power button

One circle: Cut out with a #804 pastry tip with the center cut out with a #12 pastry tip.

Cut a small piece from one side to allow the line to go through.

Place all pieces onto the control button, as shown in the photo, with tiny dabs of egg white or water.

To form a strip around the USB connector, first paint the inside of it using a mixture of metallic silver dust and lemon extract. Roll a strip of gray gum paste out to ¹⁄₁₆ inch thick and cut a ⅛ x 6-inch strip. Attach it with egg whites or water around the outside edge of the connector.

MAKE THE HEADPHONES (Optional)

This MP3 player is cute on its own but if you have the time and want to create the headphones, here's how you do it. Don't attach the phones until the cake is on its final serving platter because they are fragile and difficult to move once they are attached!

1. For each pair of headphones, you will need 1¼ ounces white gum and 1¼ ounces of light gray gum paste.

2. To create the plug that connects the headphones to the player, roll ¼ ounce of white gum paste into the shape of a small wine bottle, 1¼ inches tall and ⅜ inch wide.

3. With a toothpick, make a hole in the thinner end about ⅛ inch wide to accommodate the "wire."

4. Use ¼ ounce of light gray to form the wire splitter. Roll the gum paste out to ³⁄₁₆ inch thick and cut a 1½ x ½ inch rectangle. Cut it into the shape of a flattened wine bottle (see photo). Emboss lines around the wire splitter ¾ inch from the thinner end using a paring knife. Use a toothpick to create a hole ⅛ inch wide on the smaller end and two holes on the wider end for the wires to fit into later.

5. The earphones are made up of two discs, two domes, and two tubes. Roll out ½ ounce of the gray gum paste to about ⅛ inch thick and cut out two 1-inch circles. Next roll ½ ounce of white gum paste ¼ inch thick and cut two ⅞-inch rounds. Use your hands to form the white circles into domes with a 1-inch base. (The shape is like the top of a mushroom.) Glue the white domes to the gray 1-inch discs with a dab of egg whites. Use a toothpick to create holes around the edge of the white domed earpiece, about ⅛ inch apart (see photo).

6. Roll ½ ounce of white gum paste into two tubes about 1¾ inches long and ¼ inch wide. Round each end and make holes with a toothpick, about ¹⁄₁₆ inch wide, so the wires will fit into it later. Roll out ¼ ounce of gray gum paste paper thin and cut 2 strips to wrap around the ends of the tubes with the holes. The strips should cover about a third of the tube. Glue the tubes to the back of the domed ear pieces, a little off-center and with the gray end hanging over about ¾ inch.

7. Form the wires using a clay gun fitted with two disc attachments, ¹⁄₁₆ inch round and ¹⁄₃₂ inch round. Take ¼ ounce gray gum paste and squeeze out three 16-inch long strips, one using the ¹⁄₁₆ inch attachment and the other two using the ¹⁄₃₂ inch attachment.

8. Attach the plug you made in step #2 to the MP3 player with a small amount of egg white. Using more egg white, glue the thickest of the three wires into the plug and attach the other end into the small side of the wire splitter. Glue the two smaller wires into the wider side of the wire splitter and the other ends into the earphones. Allow the wires to drape naturally.

HOT TIP

* To save time, you could draw the controls on the MP3 player with an edible marker — and you could skip making the headphones and use real headphones instead. Just don't let anyone eat them!

Mini Cake Templates

PHOTOCOPY THESE TEMPLATES TO HELP WITH YOUR OUTLINES.

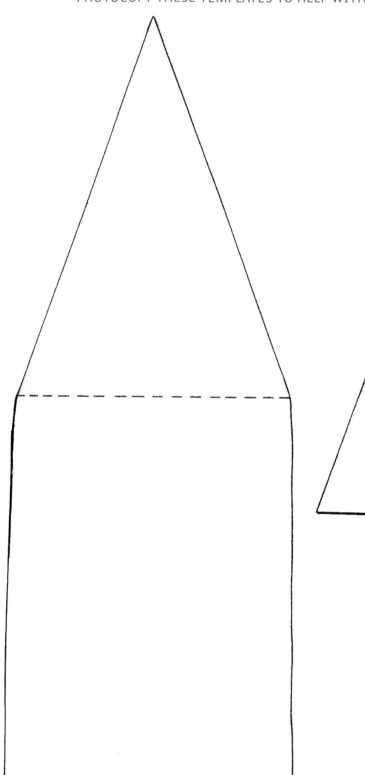

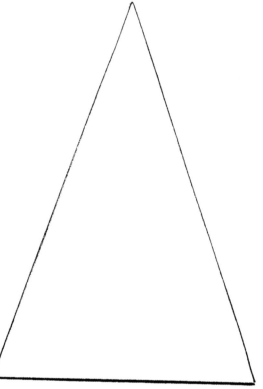

SLICE OF CAKE BROWNIE
(PAGE 135)

154

Mini Cake Templates

CONVERSATION HEART
(PAGE 138)

Cakes

· · · · · · · · · · · · · · ·

Making one of these cakes for a child close to you
means creating memories that
will last a lifetime. These are more than just cakes—
they are fun and fabulous confections
that will captivate the imagination of anyone who sees them!
I hope the projects in this chapter will
inspire you— and convince you that you truly can create
almost any object, from a
favorite backpack to a beloved childhood toy, in cake form.

· · ·

Of course, these unforgettable cakes are time-consuming and require much attention to detail.
But you can do it! When I begin an elaborate cake project, I give myself plenty of time — several
days or a week — to complete all the decorations and allow them to dry. These cakes will seem
much easier if you break up the tasks instead of trying to tackle everything at once. And I always
suggest reading the entire set of instructions thoroughly before you begin so there are no surprises
and you have everything you need.

As you work, pay close attention to the structural details. Doweling and using support boards as
directed will help ensure that your masterpiece remains solidly intact and will support all your
cute decorations. If you want to save time, do not skip the support steps — consider making fewer
decorations or serving the cake on a plate or platter instead of covering a cake base in fondant,
which we usually do. You can generally use any flavor cake you wish for these cakes, but you
should be sure to use a sturdy filling, such as one of our buttercreams or the Milk Chocolate Ganache from the Basic Recipes section (pages 71–77). These fillings hold up well to the demands of
large, sculpted cakes.

Gift Box Cake with Safari Animals

YIELD: 35 to 40 servings

Gift box cakes are one of Confetti Cakes' signature designs. We have made more gift boxes than any other shape of cake. It is not difficult to prepare if you follow the instructions carefully — and the results are impressive! We have made it for baby showers, birthdays for people of all ages, and countless other celebrations in every color of the rainbow (from hot pinks to sophisticated blues and browns) and a wide assortment of patterns. When we change the size of the polka dots and stripes, it becomes a completely original cake. And the accompanying sugar sculptures can go with almost any theme. The bow, shimmery tissue paper, and little creatures are all made from gum paste, which gives them their all-important structure. Do not substitute fondant for gum paste when making the bow.

WHAT YOU NEED

RECIPES

3 cake recipes (see Basic Recipes, pages 64–69) to make 3 half-sheet cakes, 1 inch high

1½ frosting recipes (see Basic Recipes, pages 71–77)

1 recipe Royal Icing (page 78)

MATERIALS

3¼ pounds gum paste

Food-coloring gels: leaf green, lemon yellow

Optional food-coloring gels for animals: buckeye brown, sunset orange, black, pink

Shortening (for rolling out gum paste)

Egg whites

6½ pounds fondant

Cornstarch (for rolling out fondant)

Luster dust: super pearl

EQUIPMENT

Toothpicks

Parchment paper

Plastic mat

Small rolling pin

Paring knife

Ruler

Small paintbrushes

55 cloth-covered wires, approximately 3 inches long and 22 gauge

Paper towels

Large tray

Large rolling pin

Strainer

Dry pastry brush

Fondant smoothers

One 14-inch square cake base (made from three pieces of foam core or store-bought)

Two 10-inch-square foam core boards, cut and glued together in advance for the cake base for the bottom of the gift box

Two 10-inch-square foam core boards, cut and glued together in advance for the cake base for the lid

Pastry bag and coupler

Small rubber spatula

Scissors

Small serrated knife

Offset spatula

Turntable

Round cutters: ½-inch, ⅞-inch

5 (¼-inch-wide) wooden dowels: 2 approximately 6 inches long, 3 approximately 4 inches long

Wooden skewers

Pen

Palette knife

(CONTINUED ON NEXT PAGE)

WHAT YOU NEED

EQUIPMENT (CONTINUED)

White glue

1 large dry paintbrush

Pastry tips: #2, #4, #7 (optional, for the dots on the loop bows)

Decorative ribbon

OPTIONAL EQUIPMENT FOR SUGAR ANIMALS AND PALM TREE

GIRAFFE

Veining tool

Ball tool

Pastry tips: #2, #804, #805

ELEPHANT

Ball tool

Plastic wrap

Pastry tips: #3, #5, #10

MONKEY

Pastry tips: #2, #6, #9, #804

PALM TREE

Leaf cutter, approximately 2¼ inches long

TECHNIQUES

Dyeing gum paste (page 50)

Making loop bows (page 55)

Covering cake base in fondant (page 45)

Filling cake (page 38)

Filling a pastry bag (page 26)

Crumb coating cake (page 40)

Covering cake with fondant (page 41)

Doweling sculpted cakes (page 47)

Painting with powders and dusts (page 50)

Deconstructing cakes (page 48)

METHOD

At least one week in advance: *Make the bow loops.*

1. Dye 16 ounces of gum paste pale green. Divide the green gum paste in half and cover, setting aside 8 ounces to use later.

2. Use 6 ounces of pale green gum paste to make about 55 loop bows. For detailed instructions, see Making Loop Bows (page 55).

At least two days in advance: *Make the tissue paper and decorative balls.*

TISSUE PAPER

1. Dye 1⅝ pounds of gum paste lemon yellow. Set aside 6 ounces for the balls around the bottom border and 4 ounces for polka dots, to be made later.

2. On a plastic mat greased with shortening, roll 1 pound of yellow gum paste (not all at once) into large sheets as thin as possible without tearing. Using a sharp knife, cut 25 to 30 pieces of tissue paper, no larger than 4-inch square.

3. Keep re-rolling the gum paste until you have cut it all into tissue pieces. The more you vary the size, the more realistic it will look. Cover a large tray with parchment paper and top with crumpled pieces of paper towel. Let the squares dry, uncovered, resting on the crumpled paper towels, for at least 2 days and up to 1 week.

BALLS

On a plastic mat greased with shortening, roll out the 6 ounces of yellow gum paste into a long rope, approximately ½ inch thick. Use a paring knife to cut the rope into random sized intervals, none longer than ½ inch, until you have approximately 130 pieces. Re-roll if needed until you have enough pieces. Roll the pieces into round balls and place them on parchment paper to dry, uncovered.

MAKE THE SAFARI ANIMALS
(Optional)

GIRAFFE *(at least one day in advance)*

1. Dye 3 ounces of gum paste bright yellow, ½ ounce bright orange, and ¼ ounce chocolate brown.

2. On a plastic mat greased with shortening, roll half the yellow gum paste into the shape of a horse without legs, making the neck long and thin.

3. Roll out the remaining yellow gum paste into 4 logs, approximately 2 inches long and ¼ inch thick, to

make the legs. Roll a thin rope 1½ inches long for the tail, and two small cones, ¼ inch tall, for the giraffe's horns. For the ears, roll two small pea size balls and use the sharp end of a veining tool to press into the center of the balls to form the indentations of the ears. (When you're done they should be almond shaped with a pointed end on one side.)

4. Attach the four legs, tail, horns, and ears using a small brush and dabs of egg white. Place a rolled-up piece of paper towel between the legs and a small piece to support the horns and let the giraffe dry overnight on its side. The next day, when the legs are dry and the giraffe is able to stand up on its own, you can finish the remaining details.

5. Roll the bright orange gum paste out in tiny pieces, one at a time, to make different sizes of spots. (They shouldn't be perfectly round or square — see photo.) Stick the spots to the giraffe using little dabs of egg white and the small end of the ball tool to flatten them out. Cover the entire giraffe in this manner.

6. Roll the brown gum paste out to ⅛ inch thick and use the #804 tip to cut out four circles for the hooves. Attach them to the bottoms of the legs with dabs of egg white. Use a plastic rolling pin to roll out the remaining brown gum paste even thinner (to approximately ¹⁄₁₆ inch thick) and cut out two eyes using a #2 tip and one mouth using a #805 tip. Attach the eyes and the mouth. Roll three tiny balls and attach two to the top of the horns and one to the back of the tail with dabs of egg whites, using a paintbrush.

ELEPHANT *(at least one day in advance)*

1. Dye 3 ounces of gum paste gray. Leave about ¼ ounce of white gum paste for the tusks, toes, and eyes; dye about ¼ ounce of gum paste pale pink for the inside of the ears and nose; and dye a pinch of gum paste black for the eyebrows, eyes, nostrils, and tail.

2. On a plastic mat greased with shortening, roll two 1½-inch balls for the elephant's body and head. Leave one ball for the body and shape the other ball into a cone. Pull and roll the sharp end of the cone to form the trunk. Pull the trunk to about 2½ inches long and use a paring knife to make a slit for the mouth. Attach the head to the body with egg white. Before you let the trunk dry, use the small end of a ball tool to make a hole in the end of the trunk and two small indents for the tusks, one on each side of the trunk. Dry the trunk on top of a ball of plastic wrap, at least overnight, until it hardens enough to stay up on its own.

3. Roll the remaining gray gum paste into four legs, each about 1 inch long and ⅜ inch wide. Attach the four legs to the body with a brush and dabs of egg white. Roll a thin rope approximately 2 inches long, for the tail. Attach to the back of the elephant with egg white. Roll a pinch of black gum paste into a tiny cone and attach to the end of the tail.

4. Roll out the white gum paste paper thin. Cut out two eyes using a #10 pastry tip, and cut out six circles using a #5 pastry tip. Cut the circles in half to form the hooves. Glue three half circles to the bottom of each leg with egg whites and attach the two eyes in

the same manner. With the remaining gum paste, form two small tusks by rolling two equal-size logs and shaping the points with your fingers.

5. Roll the rest of the gray gum paste out to ¹⁄₁₆ inch thick to form the ears. Cut two butterfly wing shapes about 1½ inches tall. Thin the ears with a ball tool and then roll and cut out some of the pink gum paste the same way, making the pink for the inside of the ears slightly smaller. Attach the pink inside the ears using some egg white, and pinch the ear on the side that will attach to the head. Then attach the ears to the head with egg white.

6. Cut out a tiny piece of pink gum paste to insert into the end of the trunk. Roll out a tiny amount of black gum paste and use a #3 pastry tip to cut out and attach the pupils to the eyes. Roll two tiny ropes for the eyebrows and attach. Roll two tiny balls to form nostrils on the end of the trunk and attach.

7. Attach the tusks by inserting them into the holes you made earlier and gluing with a dab of egg white.

MONKEY

These instructions are for making one monkey. Double all quantities if you plan to make two monkeys. We used two monkeys here, one seated on top of the cake and one leaning into the palm tree. Both are made the same way. Mold the arms and legs of your monkey(s) according to where it (they) will eventually sit or stand.

1. Dye 1 ounce of gum paste brown and ½ ounce flesh color. You will also need a tiny amount of white and black gum paste.

2. Roll a ball of brown gum paste the size of a large marble for the body and roll a small marble for the head. Then roll four ropes about 1¼ inches long and ¼ inch thick to form the arms and legs, and another rope slightly thinner and longer for the tail. Attach the head, limbs, and tail to the body with egg white.

3. Use the flesh color to form the stomach, ears, mouth, feet, and hands. Roll it out to 1⁄16 inch thick and cut out a small piece to fit on the monkey's stomach. Re-roll the gum paste a little thicker and use a #9 pastry tip to cut out two ears, and a #804 pastry tip to cut out two circles that you will cut in half to form the pieces for the hands and feet. Use the remaining flesh-colored gum paste to roll a small ball, about half the size of the monkey's head, to form the mouth area. Attach

the mouth area with egg white. Use a toothpick to create two nostrils on the mouth area and a belly button on the stomach. Use a scalpel or paring knife to cut a slit for the mouth.

4. Attach the feet and hands to the legs and arms with egg white.

5. Roll out a tiny piece of white and a tiny piece of black gum paste. Use a #6 pastry tip to cut out two white eyes and a #2 pastry tip to cut out pupils. Attach to the head above the mouth area. Roll two tiny pieces of black to form the eyebrows and attach them above the eyes.

PALM TREE

1. Dye ½ ounce of gum paste brown and ½ ounce moss green. Roll the brown gum paste into a cone about 4 inches long for the tree trunk. One end should be thicker then the other. Use a paring knife to make diagonal markings on the tree trunk.

2. On a plastic mat greased with shortening, roll out the moss green gum paste to 1⁄16 inch thick and cut out 8 to 10 palms using the leaf cutter. Use a paring knife to cut the edges of the palms in a diagonal pattern to make the individual blades.

3. Attach the trunk of the tree to the cake base using a brush moistened with a dab of egg white, then attach the palms to the trunk in an overlapping pattern, starting at the top of the trunk, again using egg white to attach.

CAKE BASE

Dye 2 pounds of fondant pale green. Roll out to ⅛ inch thick and cover the cake base.

MAKE AND ASSEMBLE THE CAKE

1. Prepare the cake batter and bake in 3 half-sheet pans as directed in the recipe. Let cool completely for 20 minutes, remove from pans, then wrap tightly in plastic wrap and freeze for at least one hour. (This makes the cakes easier to cut.)

2. While the cake is chilling, make the frosting and Royal Icing.

3. Cut four 10-inch squares of cake. (In order to get four squares out of three sheets of cake, you will need to piece two of the layers of cake together. So be careful to measure everything ahead of time before cutting).

4. Place a dab of filling on a square cake board and attach one layer of cake. Top the cake with ½ inch of filling, add another cake square, top that with a ½ inch of filling, and place the third cake square on top. When the top layer of cake is on, push down slightly to secure the layers.

5. Place a dab of filling on the other cake board, and place the remaining square of cake on it (for the lid).

6. Now you have two separate cakes, one about 4 inches high (for the box) and the other about 1 inch high (for the lid). Trim to square up all the edges of both cakes with a serrated knife. If the cakes are shifting as you trim, freeze them for an hour. Cut away any excess cardboard with a serrated knife or scissors.

7. Crumb coat the cakes with a very thin layer of filling.

8. On a surface lightly coated with corn-starch, roll out 3 pounds of white fondant to ¼ inch thick. Cover the three-layer cake with fondant, paying careful attention when cutting away the excess. You want completely straight edges

on all sides of the cake. Repeat the process using the remaining 1½ pounds of white fondant to cover the lid.

9. Before assembling the cake, decorate it. On a plastic mat greased with shortening, roll the remaining 8 ounces of pale green gum paste (left over from making the bows) into a sheet approximately ⅛6 inch thick. Cut it into strips ⅜ inch wide and 4½ inches long. Place the box cake on the center of a turntable, and use a small brush dipped in a little bit of water to attach the stripes vertically to the bottom, about ½ inch apart. (Don't use egg whites here because they might squeeze out from under the stripes and leave a slight yellow tint, and a super-strong hold is not required to keep the stripes in place.) Trim any excess from the top and bottom of the cake with a paring knife. Re-roll the remaining green gum paste to ⅛6 inch thick and cut out the polka dots for the lid with a ⅞-inch round cutter. Attach the dots all over the lid with water. Roll out 2 ounces of the pale yellow gum paste to ⅛6 inch thick and cut out small dots with a ½-inch round cutter (or a #806 pastry tip). Attach them to the centers of the green dots with dabs of water.

10. Place several dots of Royal Icing in the center of the cake base. Place the bottom of the gift box on the base and center it with your hands or fondant smoothers.

11. Cut the wooden dowels. You will need three dowels, each approximately 4 inches tall, along one side of the cake to support the hinged side of the lid. Insert these three dowels approximately 1 inch inside the edge of the cake, all along one side, at least 3 inches apart. Cut 2 more dowels to about 6 inches

long and insert them about 3 inches in from the corners on the opposite edge of the cake to support the open end of the lid. These two dowels should stick up at least 1 inch above the cake.

12. To attach the lid of the gift box, create a line of Royal Icing along the edge of the box where you inserted the three dowels, and a dab of Royal Icing on top of the two dowels that are sticking out (see diagram). Rest one edge of the lid against the side of the cake with the three dowels and let the other edge of the lid sit right on top of the two dowels sticking out of the cake. The lid should be at an incline, with an opening about 2½ inches on one side. Allow about 10 minutes for the icing to set.

13. Before adding the tissue paper, dust both sides of all the tissue paper pieces with pearl luster dust, using a dry brush. The dust tends to float into the air, so work away from the cake when dusting.

14. Using stiff Royal Icing in a pastry bag fitted with a #4 tip, attach all the pieces of tissue paper, placing pieces between the box and the lid one at a time. Fill in the entire area so you cannot see through.

15. Attach the yellow balls around the bottom edge of the cake using tiny dabs of Royal Icing from a pastry bag fitted with a #2 tip as glue. (You can use

the same pastry bag you used to attach the tissue, fitted with a smaller tip.)

16. If desired, you can decorate the loop bows further by adding tiny polka dots before attaching them to the cake. This is time-consuming and optional; a plain bow will still look beautiful. To make the dots, roll out any remaining yellow gum paste (you should have at least 2 ounces left) as thin as possible on a surface coated in shortening. Cut out dots using the small end of a #7 pastry tip. Attach the dots to the bows in a random pattern with dabs of water. You will need roughly 30 dots per loop.

17. Roll out a ½-inch ball of white gum paste. Attach it to the center of the top of the cake with a drop of water. Insert the wire ends of the dried loop bows, one at a time, through the ball and into the center of the cake. If the wires are too long, snip them with scissors. Fill the entire ball with loop bows, starting with one loop bow pointing straight up in the very center and working around the center bow to the outside, creating a full rounded bow. (If you are having difficulty getting the loops through the center ball, use a thin skewer to pierce a hole before pushing the loop in.)

18. Use white glue to attach a decorative ribbon around the cake base.

Candy Factory Cake

YIELD: 35 to 40 servings

We first made a cake like this for a five-year-old's birthday party with a Willy Wonka–inspired theme. The tiers of cake are covered in chocolate fondant and then topped with a layer of green fondant "grass" to give the look of the banks along Willy Wonka's chocolate river. To create a more intense chocolate sensation, spread melted chocolate to cover the base instead of the colorful rock candy.

WHAT YOU NEED

RECIPES

2 cake recipes (see Basic Recipes, pages 64–69) to make two 6-inch round cakes and two 10-inch round cakes, all 2 inches high

2 frosting recipes (see Basic Recipes, pages 71–77)

1 recipe Royal Icing (page 78)

MATERIALS

2 cups vodka

Food-coloring gels: violet, purple, rose pink, electric pink, lemon yellow, royal blue, sunset orange, leaf green

3 pounds rock candy

2½ pounds gum paste

Shortening (for rolling out gum paste)

Lemon extract

Luster dusts: rose pink, cotton candy

Egg whites

Edible yellow glitter

5 pounds chocolate fondant

Cornstarch (for rolling out fondant)

2¼ pounds fondant

Food-coloring powder: green

EQUIPMENT

Metal bowl (for dyeing rock candy)

Strainer (for dyeing rock candy)

Trays (for dyeing rock candy)

Parchment paper

Toothpicks

Plastic mat

Small and large rolling pins

Letter cutters (for THE CANDY FACTORY), approximately 3 inches high and 2 inches wide, or templates (page 210)

Scalpel

Set of round cutters (with 12 cutters)

15 lollipop sticks, approximately five ⅛-inch thick and ten ³⁄₁₆-inch thick

5-petal blossom cutter(s) (for bursting-flower lollipops)

Small and large paintbrushes

Pastry Tips: #2, #804, #805, #808

Paper towels

Scissors

Pastry bags and couplers

Small rubber spatula

Small and large serrated knives

Ruler

Two round cake boards, 6-inch and 10-inch, made from foam core or two pieces of cardboard cut and glued together in advance

Offset spatula(s)

Strainer (for rolling out fondant)

(CONTINUED ON NEXT PAGE)

METHOD

At least two days to one week in advance:
Make the decorations.

ROCK CANDY

1. To dye the rock candy, combine the vodka and ¼ teaspoon each of the violet and purple food coloring in a metal bowl. Stir to distribute the food coloring evenly.

2. Place a handful of rock candy crystals in a strainer and lower the strainer into the vodka mixture. After a few seconds, remove the strainer from the bowl, allowing the excess liquid to drain back into the bowl. If the color is too dark, add more vodka or water to lighten it. The longer you keep the strainer in the mixture, the darker the crystals will become.

3. Spread the dyed rock candy crystals in a single layer on a tray lined with parchment paper and let dry overnight.

4. Repeat with the rest of the rock candy crystals.

LETTERS

1. Dye approximately 1 pound of gum paste pink. On a plastic mat greased with shortening, roll the pink gum paste out to ⅜ inch thick. Use the letter cutters to cut out THE CANDY FACTORY (or use the templates on page 210). You could also personalize the cake with a name, HAPPY BIRTHDAY, or another sentiment.

2. Trim each letter with a scalpel and use your fingers (coated with shortening) to smooth out the sides and edges. Allow the letters to dry for at least 2 days.

3. When the letters are firm, paint them with a mixture of lemon extract and rose pink luster dust. Paint the front and back of each letter. Let dry for a few hours and then dust lightly with cotton candy luster dust (not using any extract or liquid) to give them a pale pink shimmer.

LOLLIPOPS

1. Divide approximately 1¼ pounds gum paste into five portions (4 ounces each). Dye one portion pale pink, one pale yellow, one lilac, one orange, and one pale blue.

2. On a plastic mat greased with shortening, roll out one color at a time to approximately ¼ inch thick. Use different sizes of round cutters to cut at least three circles of each color. Here we used 1½-inch, 1⅞-inch, 2¼-inch, and 2⅞-inch cutters, but any size circles will look great!

3. Insert a paper lollipop stick into the bottom of each circle. Use the ½-inch sticks in the larger circles and ³⁄₁₆-inch sticks in the smaller ones. After you make an indent, pull out the stick, brush it with egg white, and reinsert it about halfway into the circle. Leave the lollipop sticks different lengths. Let the lollipops dry for at least 2 days before decorating.

4. To decorate, we used a few different designs. Have fun and let your imagination run wild. Use a variety of round cutters or pastry tips to make unique designs. We dyed less than 1 ounce of gum paste for each decorative color used. You could also use any leftovers from the gum paste you used to make the lollipops. Here are a few of our favorite designs:

SPIRAL: Roll out a strip of gum paste (in a contrasting color to the lollipop background) about 1/16 inch wide and 4 inches long (or longer for a large lollipop), and as thin as possible. Cut each end to a point. Brush a lollipop lightly with egg white and create a spiral, starting in the middle in a tight swirl and moving out toward the edge, following the shape of the circle.

PINWHEEL: Roll out a piece of gum paste as thin as possible and large enough to cut out a circle slightly larger than the lollipop. Cut out a circle with a round cutter and divide it into 14 wedge-shaped sections (as if you were cutting a pizza). Brush the surface of a lollipop with egg white and attach every other section of the circle onto the lollipop, starting in the center and overlapping the points.

BURSTING FLOWER: These colorful pops are made using different colors of gum paste cut out with 5-petal blossom cutters. Cut out blossoms from gum paste rolled as thin as possible, and then cut the blossoms into individual petal sections. Use egg white to glue the individual petals onto a lollipop in a circle pattern. Cut centers for the bursting flowers with a small round cutter or pastry tip. Accent the individual petals with different sizes of dots cut with various pastry tips or the petals from another small, divided blossom cutout. As you create a pattern, remember that the design should be circular and symmetrical.

STEP STONES

1. For the glitter-covered stones that will adorn the cake base, dye approximately 2 ounces of gum paste hot pink. Roll the gum paste to 1/2 inch thick and cut out 20 circles using different sizes of round cutters and round pastry tips. Here we used #804, #805, and #808 tips, and 7/8-inch, 1¼-inch, and 1½-inch cutters.

2. Allow the circles to dry overnight and then brush the tops with egg white and sprinkle yellow edible glitter over them. Shake off the excess.

CANDY DOTS

1. Roll out 1 ounce of white gum paste as thin as possible. Cut a few strips approximately 2 inches wide and 6 inches long. Lay the strips over some paper towels to achieve a rippled effect. Let dry overnight.

2. Make 1 recipe Royal Icing. Use ½ cup here and reserve the rest. Divide the ½ cup into three portions and dye one portion hot pink, one bright yellow, and one deep turquoise. Fill pastry bags fitted with #2 tips with each color. Pipe three rows of three dots each on the dried strips of white gum paste and then switch colors. Let them dry for at least one hour so the dots have time to harden.

8 inches at the bottom. Then carve a slight slant to the top of each tier. If you look at the cakes at eye level, one side should be 6 inches high, with the top slanting down to 4 inches high at the other side. Once the cakes are completely sculpted, cut away any excess cardboard with a serrated knife or scissors. Crumb coat the cakes with a thin layer of filling. Put them back in the refrigerator to chill while you roll out the fondant.

6. Divide the chocolate fondant and into two portions, one 2 pounds (for the 6-inch tier) and the other 3 pounds (for the 10-inch tier). Chocolate fondant can be slightly softer than vanilla fondant — and that's fine. Roll out the chocolate fondant to ¼ inch thick and cover each tier.

7. Dye the 2¼ pounds of white fondant green (or use store-bought green fondant). Roll 12 ounces out to ⅛ inch thick at the edges, leaving the center thicker, about ½ inch thick. (The shape of the fondant should resemble a fried egg.) Cut out an 8-inch circle that will slightly overhang the 6-inch tier. Place the circle on the top tier and gently press the fondant into small mounds with your fingers — it should resemble uneven grassy land. Thin the edges by pulling the green fondant slightly with your fingers, and then use scissors to cut the edges into blades of grass. Repeat for the 10-inch tier, using about 1½ pounds of green fondant cut to a 12-inch circle. But instead of making a mound in the center, flatten the space in the middle so the smaller tier can sit flat on it, then create the mounds around this area. Use any

MAKE AND ASSEMBLE THE CAKE

1. Prepare the cake batter, pour it into two 6-inch and two 10-inch round pans (at least 2 inches high), and bake according to the recipe. Let cool for 20 minutes, remove from pans, then wrap tightly in plastic wrap and freeze for at least one hour. (This makes the cakes easier to cut.)

2. While the cakes are chilling, make the filling.

3. Trim off the tops of the cakes. Split each cake into two 1-inch layers. You will be making one tier 6 inches in diameter and one tier 10 inches in diameter; both will be about 6 inches high when completed.

4. Create the tiers one at a time on their cake boards. Stack the layers, filling them with ½-inch layers of filling. Each tier should have 4 layers of cake and 3 layers of filling. When the top tier is on, press gently to secure the layers. Place the cakes in the refrigerator and chill for at least an hour until they are firm. This will make the cakes easier to carve.

5. Using large and small serrated knives, carve the cakes so they slope up on the sides. The cakes should be wider at the top and smaller at the bottom. The 6-inch round tier should be 6 inches wide at top and taper to 4 inches at the bottom. The 10-inch tier should taper from 10 inches wide on top to

leftover green fondant to form a small green "island" that you will place in front of the cake on the base (see photo on page 164). Thin the edges of the island and cut blades of grass as you did for the green fondant on top of the tiers.

8. Before inserting dowels into the bottom tier, dust the top of both cakes with a thin layer of green food coloring powder using a dry pastry brush. Dust the fondant island with the green food-coloring powder and set it aside to use later.

9. Cover your wacky-shaped cake base with foil and secure the foil with tape. Make sure the foil is completely flat on the bottom so the base will sit flat. Use white glue to attach decorative ribbon around the base before you decorate.

10. Use Royal Icing to glue the 10-inch tier, slightly off-center, onto the base. Let it set for at least 10 minutes.

11. Cut and insert three plastic dowels into the 10-inch tier, forming a triangle in the center. Cut the dowels to the same angle as the top of the bottom tier; you may need to cut on a diagonal. Stay within a 4-inch radius so you will not see the dowels once the top tier is placed on top. Make sure to place two of the three dowels on the shorter side of the cake (the side where the cake is sloped to 4 inches) to ensure that the top tier will be completely stable. Attach the 6-inch tier on top of the 10-inch tier with Royal Icing, making sure the taller side of the cake is in the back.

12. Sharpen the end of the wooden dowel. Measure the height of the cake from the base to the top tier and cut the dowel to be slightly shorter then the entire cake. Hammer the sharpened dowel into the center of the top tier until it goes through both tiers (the sharpened end will cut through the cake boards to the bottom). This dowel will prevent the cake from shifting. Fill in the hole in the top with a small amount of the leftover green fondant.

13. Dye half of the reserved Royal Icing the color of the dyed rock candy. Spread the icing onto the base with a small offset spatula, working in one small area at a time. Working quickly, attach the green island in front of the cake and then add the rock candy. Cover the entire base with Royal Icing and rock candy.

14. Attach the letters with toothpicks and a small amount of Royal Icing on the bottom of each letter. Insert toothpicks about halfway up into the letters that will sit on top of tiers of cake (those that will sit in front of the bottom tier on the cake base do not need toothpicks) and insert the other ends of the toothpicks into the cake. For the letters in the bottom row, simply attach with Royal Icing.

15. Attach the step stones and candy dots to the base with Royal Icing.

16. Insert the lollipop sticks directly into the cake (and island) at various levels.

17. Once all the letters are placed on the cake, pipe small yellow dots of Royal Icing onto them using a pastry bag fitted with a #2 tip.

Quinceañera Cake

A Quinceañera is a celebration of a young woman's fifteenth birthday, inspired by the traditions of Latin America and South America. This is the perfect cake for the princess in your life — for her fifteenth birthday, sweet-sixteen party, christening, bat mitzvah, or any very special occasion. The gold tiara and brush embroidery on the cake make it pretty and glamorous. Feel free to use our patterns here, or create your own based on your favorite porcelain, china, or lace. This cake can be made in all different sizes and shapes. For a cake that looks just like the one pictured here, you will need two petal-shaped pans, but if you do not have them, round or square tiers would look just as beautiful.

WHAT YOU NEED

RECIPES

7 cake recipes (see Basic Recipes, pages 64–69) to make one 5-inch round cake, one 8-inch round cake, one 12-inch petal cake, and one 15-inch petal cake, all 3 inches high

6 frosting recipes (see Basic Recipes, pages 71–77)

1 recipe Royal Icing (page 78)

MATERIALS

4 ounces gum paste (for tiara)

Shortening (for rolling out gum paste)

Egg whites

Metallic gold dust

Lemon extract

14 pounds fondant

Food-coloring gels: rose pink, avocado, super red, violet

Cornstarch (for rolling out fondant)

Luster dust: six 4-gram containers super pearl

Petal dust: three 4-gram containers cosmos pink

Approximately 40 store-bought edible pearls

EQUIPMENT

Tiara template (page 212)

Parchment paper

Plastic mat

Small rolling pin

Ruler

Paring knife

Small and large paintbrushes

4-inch round, 3-inch high cake pan (for drying tiara)

Toothpicks

One 18-inch petal-shaped cake base (made from wood or store-bought; see template, page 213)

Petal-shaped pans: 12-inch, 15-inch

2 **round** cake boards, one 5-inch and one 8-inch, made from foam core or two pieces of cardboard cut and glued together in advance

2 **petal** cake boards, one 12-inch and one 15-inch, made from foam core or two pieces of cardboard cut and glued together in advance

Scissors

Pastry bags and couplers

Pastry tips: #1, #2, #3

Small rubber spatula

Large and small serrated knives

Offset spatula(s)

Large rolling pin

(CONTINUED ON NEXT PAGE)

WHAT YOU NEED

EQUIPMENT (CONTINUED)

Strainer

Dry pastry brush

Fondant smoothers

18 plastic dowels, approximately
4 inches long and ¾ inch wide

1 wooden dowel, approximately
16 inches long and ¼ inch wide

Wooden skewers

Pen

Palette knife

Pencil sharpener

Mallet or hammer

Templates for piping patterns
(page 174)

White glue

Decorative gold ribbon

TECHNIQUES

Dyeing fondant and gum paste
(page 50)

Covering cake base in fondant
(page 45)

Splitting cake (page 36)

Filling a pastry bag (page 26)

Filling cake (page 38)

Crumb coating cake (page 40)

Covering cake with fondant
(page 41)

Doweling sculpted cakes (page 47)

Painting with luster dusts (page 50)

Deconstructing cakes (page 48)

METHOD

At least three days to one week in advance:
Make the tiara.

1. Trace the tiara template (page 212) on a piece of parchment paper approximately 14 inches wide and 3 inches tall.

2. Turn the parchment over so the pencil doesn't get on the gum paste and place it on a flat work surface.

3. Roll the 4 ounces of gum paste out on a plastic mat greased with shortening to ⅛ inch thick. Cut one ¼ x 12¾-inch strip for the base of the tiara and align it with the bottom of your template. Cut the remaining gum paste into strips ⅛ inch wide and varying lengths to fit the tiara template. The two sides of the tiara should be symmetrical. Place the strips on the template and form the curls and the teardrop shape at the top. As you add each strip, attach it to the base and to adjacent strips using a small brush and dabs of egg white. Trim all pieces to fit the template.

4. Once all the strips are on the template, carefully wrap the tiara with the parchment paper around a 4-inch round, 3-inch high cake pan to dry. After a few days the tiara will be dry and you can peel the parchment paper away.

5. Paint the entire tiara, front and back, with a mixture of metallic gold dust and lemon extract.

At least two days in advance: *Make the cake base.*

Dye all the fondant pale pink (we used rose-pink food coloring). Roll out approximately 4 pounds of fondant to ⅛ inch thick and use it to cover the cake base. Wrap the remaining fondant with plastic and keep in an airtight container until you are ready to cover the cakes.

MAKE AND ASSEMBLE THE CAKE

1. Prepare the cake batter, pour into the pans specified, and bake according to the recipe. Let the cakes cool completely, approximately 20 minutes. Remove from pans, wrap tightly in plastic wrap, and freeze for at least one hour. This will make them easier to cut.

2. While the cake is chilling, make the filling and the Royal Icing.

3. Split each cake into three 1-inch layers. (When you add filling, all the tiers will be 4 inches high.)

4. Create the tiers one at a time on their cake boards. Attach the first layer to its board with a dab of filling. Coat the layer with ½ inch of filling, add the next layer, coat with another ½ inch of filling, and add the top layer. Each tier will have 3 layers of cake and 2 layers of filling. When the top tier is on, press gently to secure the layers. Crumb coat each tier with a very thin layer of filling.

5. Roll out the pink fondant to ¼ inch thick and cover each tier. See the fondant chart on page 81 to determine how much you will need for each tier. On this cake, we left the edges of the fondant slightly rounded on purpose to give a softer look.

6. Use Royal Icing to glue the 15-inch tier in the center of the base. Let it set for at least 10 minutes.

7. Insert 9 of the 4-inch plastic dowels into the 15-inch tier. Put 1 in the center and surround it with a circle of 8 dowels. Stay within an 11-inch radius so you will not see the dowels once the 12-inch tier is placed on top. Continue in this manner and place the 12-inch tier on top of the 15-inch

tier with Royal Icing. Dowel this tier with 6 dowels and the 8-inch tier with 3 dowels. End with the 5-inch tier on top. (There will be no plastic dowels in the top tier.)

8. Before you begin to decorate, sharpen the end of the wooden dowel and measure the height from the cake from the base to the top tier. Trim the dowel so it is slightly shorter than the entire cake. Hammer the dowel, sharpened end down, into the center of the top tier until it goes through all of the layers. The sharpened end will cut through the cake boards to the bottom. This dowel will prevent the cake from shifting. Fill in the hole in

the top tier with a small amount of the leftover pink fondant.

9. Once the cake is completely tiered, use a mixture of super pearl luster dust, cosmos-pink petal dust, and lemon extract, and paint the entire cake with a large brush. The intensity of the color will depend on the consistency of your paint mixture.

10. Let the cake dry for at least 10 minutes, then use a pastry bag fitted with a #2 tip to pipe a border of white Royal Icing dots about ⅛ inch apart around the bottom edge of each tier.

11. Change the tip of the pastry bag filled with white icing to a #3. Enlarge the piping patterns on page 174 by photocopying them at 135 and 145 percent, respectively. With a pen, trace the enlarged piping patterns onto parchment paper. Either use a toothpick to follow the pattern and emboss the design onto the cake, or use a pencil rubbing to transfer the design. To transfer the design with a pencil rubbing, trace the enlarged design with pencil (pressing firmly) onto parchment paper. Turn the penciled side of the parchment paper onto the fondant-covered cake, making sure the design is right-side-up. Rub the back of the paper gently against the fondant with a rounded point. The rubbing will come off onto the cake and you will be able to follow the design when piping. Pipe the patterns on each tier in white icing. Let them dry for at least one hour. With a small paintbrush, use a mixture of gold dust and lemon extract to paint all of the piping.

12. To make the cherries, dye about 3 tablespoons of Royal Icing green with about 2 drops of avocado food coloring. Dye another 3 tablespoons of Royal Icing cherry red using super red with a touch of violet food coloring. Fill a pastry bag fitted with a #1 tip with the green icing; fill a bag fitted with a #2 tip with the red icing. For the flowers, fill a pastry bag fitted with a #3 pastry tip with white icing.

CHERRIES: Pipe two lines for the stems and a leaf with the green icing. For the leaf shape apply pressure at the beginning and then gradually release pressure to achieve the leaf shape from thick to thin. Use the red icing and pipe approximately 9 dots on each section to create a group of cherries.

desired size is 5¾" x 3" (enlarge by 135%)

desired size is 3" x 3" (enlarge by 145%)

BRUSH EMBROIDERY TECHNIQUE FOR FLOWERS

FLOWERS: The flowers use some simple piping and a technique called brush embroidery. Brush embroidery allows you to create the delicate look of hand-painted porcelain. Pipe the green stem of the flower and then pipe the outline of the petals in the white icing. Dip a small brush in water or egg whites and pull the icing from the line toward the center of the flower petals in one smooth stroke, so the color is thickest at the line and fades to a thin transparency in the middle of the petals (see illustration). Use the same method for the leaves, pulling the icing from the outside of the leaf edge to the center. Pipe overlapping dots in white Royal Icing to create the extra blossoms on the stems. To finish the pattern, pipe four dots in red icing in a diamond pattern on the outside edge of the design.

14. Attach the tiara to the top of the cake with Royal Icing. To embellish the cake further, attach edible sugar pearls along the base of the tiara and between the cherry designs on the second tier from the top.

15. Use white glue to attach a decorative gold ribbon around the cake base.

HOT TIP

* For the brush embroidery technique to work properly the Royal Icing should be thin enough that it can be brushed smoothly yet thick enough to hold its shape. If it's too thin, add stiff icing or confectioners' sugar.

Toy Train Cake

Every two-, three-, and four-year old I know is fascinated with things that move, especially trains, buses, and fire engines. This is a fantastic birthday cake for kids in that age range (or any child who loves trains). It can also be great for a baby shower, especially if you change the colors to pastels. (Think "baby on board!") Personalize the cake by placing the number of the birthday child's age on the side of the train. To save time, instead of decorating the base to look like a wooden floor, spread crushed chocolate cookies on a base or serving platter for the look of coals on a railroad track, gluing them on with a thin layer of loose Royal Icing. Don't feel daunted by the scope of this project: This cake looks more difficult to make than it is. It's made from three different shapes: a short rectangle for the base, a tall rectangle for the cabin, and a cylinder for the front engine.

WHAT YOU NEED

RECIPES

2 cake recipes (see Basic Recipes, pages 64–69) to make two half-sheet cakes, 1 inch high

1 frosting recipe (see Basic Recipes, pages 71–77)

½ recipe Royal Icing (page 78)

MATERIALS

4 pounds gum paste

Food-coloring gels: lemon yellow, royal blue, super red, coal black, buckeye brown (optional, for cake base)

Shortening (for rolling out gum paste)

Egg whites

½ cup vodka (optional, for cake base)

6½ pounds rolled fondant, includes 3 pounds for the optional cake base, (store-bought or page 80)

Cornstarch (for rolling out fondant)

EQUIPMENT

Toothpicks

Plastic mat

Small and large rolling pins

Round cutters: ⅝-inch (optional), ¾-inch, ⅞-inch, 1-inch, 1⅞-inch, 2-inch, 2½-inch, 3¾-inch

Paring knife

Scalpel or veining tool

Pastry tips: #6, #10, #12, #804, #808

Ruler

One 14 x 18-inch cake base (made from 3 layers of foam core or store-bought, optional)

1 large wide paintbrush with stiff bristles (optional, for cake base)

Small paintbrushes

Small and large serrated knives

Drafting triangle

3 cake boards, made from one layer each of foam core, cut in advance for each section of the cake: one 9 x 4-inch rectangle for the base, one 6 x 1-inch rectangle for the engine, and one 6 x 1½-inch rectangle for the cabin

Scissors

Small rubber spatula

X-acto knife

Offset spatula(s)

Pastry bag and coupler

Strainer (for rolling out fondant)

Dry pastry brush

One 9½ x 5-inch support board made from 2 pieces of foam core cut and glued together in advance

Fondant smoothers

3 plastic dowels, approximately 6 inches long and ¾ inch wide

White glue

Decorative ribbon

(CONTINUED ON NEXT PAGE)

METHOD

At least three days to one week in advance:
Make the wheels and smokestack.
I suggest dyeing all the gum paste colors ahead of time. Double wrap them in plastic and set aside until you are ready to use. Saturated colors such as black and red tend to require a lot of food coloring, and are often extra soft. If you find the gum paste is too soft to work with, add sifted confectioners' sugar into the dough a little at a time. Knead until the dough is pliable but not sticky.

Dye 13 ounces of gum paste black, 2 pounds yellow, and 1 pound red. Reserve a pea-size amount of white gum paste.

WHEELS

1. Roll out 12 ounces of black gum paste on a plastic mat lightly coated with shortening to ½ inch thick. Use a 1⁷/₈-inch round cutter to cut out six wheels. If you find the cutter getting stuck in the black gum paste, apply shortening to the edge of the cutter before you cut out the circles.

2. Coat your fingertips with shortening and smooth the edges of the circles. Allow the circles to dry overnight before decorating.

3. Once the wheels are firm to the touch, roll out 3 ounces of the yellow gum paste to ¹/₁₆ inch thick. Cut six 6 x ³/₁₆-inch strips. Attach the strips around the perimeter of the surface of each black wheel using egg whites.

4. Use the same yellow gum paste to cut out the stripes for the spokes of each wheel. For each wheel you will need eight ¾ x ⅛-inch strips. Attach the spokes inside the perimeter of the yellow edge with egg whites. Trim any excess spoke in the center of the wheel so the wheel's center may sit flat.

5. Roll out 4 ounces of red gum paste to ¹/₁₆ inch thick. Cut six 6¼ x ¾-inch strips. Attach the strips with egg whites to the outside edges of the wheels. Cover the line on the perimeter where the black and yellow come together, making sure the edge of the red strip is flush with the yellow rim.

6. Create the wheels' centers by rolling about 1 ounce each of the yellow and red gum paste (using excess gum paste from the red and yellow wheel details) out to ¼ inch thick. Cut 6 yellow circles using a #804 pastry tip and 6 red circles using a #10 tip.

7. Attach a yellow circle to the center of each wheel with egg whites then attach a red circle to the center of each yellow circle. Let dry for at least 2 days.

SMOKESTACK

1. Roll approximately 4 ounces of yellow gum paste into a cone. Use a paring knife to trim the top and bottom edges so they are flat. Once trimmed, the stack should be about 3 inches tall, 1 inch wide at the base, and 2 inches wide at the top. Use your fingers to pinch the edges to make them sharp. Wrap any unused gum paste tightly and save it to use later.

2. As soon as you have formed the smokestack, before the gum paste begins to dry, create the face. Use a sharp scalpel or veining tool to emboss the mouth just below the middle of the smokestack. Emboss two dimples.

3. Roll a pea-size ball of the yellow gum paste for the nose and attach it above the center of the mouth with egg white.

4. Roll out a pea-size amount of white gum paste so that it is paper thin and cut out 2 eyes using a #10 pastry tip. Attach the eyes to the smokestack with egg whites.

5. Roll out ½ ounce of black gum paste paper thin and cut two pupils using a #6 pastry tip. Attach the pupils to the eyes on the smokestack with a small dab of egg whites.

6. From the same black gum paste cut out a circle using a 2-inch round cutter and attach it to the top of the smokestack with egg whites.

7. Use the leftover yellow gum paste from Step 1 and roll it into a strip that is ¼ inch thick, 7 inches long, and ¼ inch wide. Apply egg whites around the top edge of the smokestack and wrap this strip around the stack, trimming with a paring knife or scalpel for a straight seam. Let the stack dry until you are ready to attach it to the cake.

At least one day in advance: *Make the cake base (optional).*

1. Dye 1 pound of fondant light brown. Twist the brown fondant with 2 pounds of white fondant. Follow the directions on page 51 for the wood staining technique.

2. Roll out the twisted brown and white fondant to slightly thicker than ⅛ inch and cover the cake base with it.

3. Use a ruler and a paring knife to mark off seven 2-inch intervals along the shorter sides of the base. Cut all the way through the fondant, creating 7 rows. Divide the sections into what will look like wooden floor panels by marking off the horizontal rows of wood with vertical markings in random patterns, cut all the way through the fondant. Think of the cake base as a piece of an actual wooden floor and imagine each panel of wood is 2 inches wide and 9 inches long. Each section should begin and end at different points (see photo on page 183).

4. Once your "wooden floor" has all its panels sectioned off, stain your board with a mixture of ½ teaspoon of brown food-coloring gel and ½ cup of vodka, using a large paintbrush with stiff bristles. After the entire board is stained go back and add finer details with a small paintbrush.

MAKE ALL THE PARTS OF THE CAKE

1. Prepare the cake batter and bake in 2 half-sheet pans as directed in the recipe. Let the cakes cool for 20 minutes, remove from pans, wrap tightly in plastic wrap, and freeze for at least 1 hour. (This makes the cakes easier to cut.)

2. While the cake is chilling, make the filling and Royal Icing.

3. From the two half-sheets, cut the 8 pieces of cake that you will use to build the 3 sections of the train (base, cabin, and cylinder). Use a small serrated knife, a ruler, and a drafting triangle to help you cut perfect angles. From the first half-sheet, cut three 5 x 3-inch rectangles and two 6 x 3-inch rectangles. From the other sheet cut two 4 x 9-inch rectangles and one 6 x 3-inch rectangle.

4. Create the sections of cake one at a time on their cake boards, as directed below. Stack the layers and, with a pastry bag, fill with ½-inch layers of filling. When the top layer of cake is on each section, press gently to secure the layers. The **base** of the train will have two 4 x 9-inch layers of cake and 1 layer of filling. Once built it should be 2 inches high, 4 inches wide, and 9 inches long. The **cabin** of the train will have three 5 x 3-inch layers of cake and 2 layers of filling. Once built, the cabin should be 4 inches high, 5 inches wide, and 3 inches deep. The **cylinder** will have three 6 x 3-inch layers of cake and 2 layers of filling. Before it's carved, the cylinder should be a flat rectangle on the bottom and measure 3 inches high, 3 inches wide, and 6 inches long. Place the stacked and filled cakes in the refrigerator to chill for at least an hour until they are firm. This will make the cakes easier to carve.

5. Use large and small serrated knives to carve the cakes. The base of the train and the cabin should simply be squared on all sides; all the sides should be perfectly straight. For the cylinder, start by slicing off the top two long edges of the block of cake. Carve a little at a time, rounding the top of the cake, and continue cutting away the bottom of the cake to round the bottom half. When you are finished you will have a cylinder with two flat ends on the front and back, rounded top and sides, and a rounded bottom with a 1½-inch flat section along the middle of the bottom.

6. Once the cakes are completely sculpted, cut away any excess cardboard with a serrated knife or scissors. Crumb coat the cakes with a thin layer of filling. Put them in the refrigerator to chill while you roll out the fondant.

7. Divide 3½ pounds of fondant into two pieces, one 3 pounds and one ½ pound. Dye the larger portion blue and dye the smaller portion red.

8. Remove the cakes from the refrigerator and cover them one at a time. Roll out 1 pound of the blue fondant to ¼ inch thick on a surface dusted with cornstarch and use it to cover the base of the train. Roll out another 1 pound and use it to cover the cabin. Roll out ¾ pound blue fondant to cover the 9½ x 5-inch foam core support board. Brush the board with piping gel or water before covering. Wrap and save the remaining blue fondant for later use. (You should have about ¼ pound or 4 ounces left over.)

9. Roll out the red fondant to ¼ inch thick on a surface dusted with cornstarch and use it to cover the cylinder-shaped cake.

10. Once the major components of the train are covered with fondant, you will need to make two more pieces before putting it all together and adding the finishing details. To make the roof that sits on top of the cabin cake, roll out 1 pound of yellow gum paste into a slab about 1⅛ inches thick. Cut out a 5¾ x 3½-inch rectangle. Use a small rolling pin and fondant smoothers to slope the short sides of the roof. The slope should begin 1¼ inches in from the edge on both sides. After the angles are sloped, re-trim the roof with a paring knife to make it 5¾ x 3½ inches and to create a straight edge on all sides (it will have stretched). Set the roof aside.

11. The part of the train that sticks out from the front is called a wedge plow. To create one for this train, roll 6 ounces of yellow gum paste into a ball then shape it into a block that is 2¼ inches tall, 4 inches wide, and 2 inches deep. Use a combination of your hands and a paring knife to form the block into a wedge that is straight across the back and has four sloped sides in the front (see photo). The two front sides should be slightly larger than the other two sides on the ends. When complete, the wedge should be 4 inches wide at the base, 3 inches wide at top, 2¼ inches tall, 1¼ inches deep at the top center, and 2 inches deep at the bottom center. Use a #6 pastry tip and emboss each corner to resemble rivets.

ASSEMBLE THE CAKE
(see photo on page 183)

1. Use the Royal Icing to glue the base of the train slightly off-center on the "wooden" cake base (or an alternate platter). Let it set for at least 5 minutes.

2. Cut and insert 3 plastic dowels into the base tier, forming a straight line in the center of the cake. Place 2 of the 3 dowels toward the front of the train cake and the third dowel at the back of the train, underneath where the cabin cake will be placed. This will ensure that the top tier is completely stable. Attach the fondant-covered support board to the top of the bottom tier with Royal Icing, making sure the support board is centered over the bottom cake and slightly overhangs the front and back.

3. Place the cabin cake toward the back of the support board; align it from the side with the bottom cake. Glue it onto the support board with Royal Icing.

4. Attach the cylinder cake to the front of the cabin along the center of the support board; it should come just to the front edge of the support board.

5. Roll 8 ounces of red gum paste out to ⅝ inch thick. Cut two ½ x 9¾-inch strips and attach them to the sides of the blue support board with egg whites. The ends of the red strips should be flush with the ends of the board. Cut another strip, ½ x 6 inches, and attach it to the back edge of the support board. Cut a final strip, ⅛ x 6 inches, and attach it to the front edge of the support board with egg whites.

6. Use Royal Icing to attach the 6 wheels to the sides of the cake, underneath the support board.

7. Roll 1 ounce of yellow gum paste out to ⅛ inch thick and cut a rectangle to fit the front of the base of the train, about 4 inches wide and 2 inches tall. Attach it to the front of the bottom cake with egg whites. Use a #6 tip to emboss rivets in the top corners of the rectangle.

8. Attach the wedge plow to the yellow rectangle on the front of the train, centered under the support board, with Royal Icing or egg whites. After the plow is in place, roll 1 ounce of red gum paste out to ⅛ inch thick and cut a piece the same shape as

the top of the wedge, but to fit ⅛ inch inside the top of the wedge. Align the long edge of this red piece against the red strip on the front of the train and attach with egg whites.

9. From the rolled out red gum paste cut fourteen ⅛ x 1½-inch strips and attach them along the four front sides of the plow (see photo).

10. Before attaching the roof and smokestack, finish the details. Roll out about 1 ounce of red gum paste to 1/16 inch thick and use a paring knife or scalpel to cut four 6½ x 3/16-inch strips for the roof. Attach the strips onto the roof with a touch of egg whites (**do not** use too much liquid or the red will bleed). Place one strip ⅜ inch from the front edge of the roof and the next strip ¼ inch away from that. Repeat near the back edge of the roof.

11. For the smokestack, cut a strip from the red gum paste about ¼ inch wide and 8 inches long. Wrap the strip around the top rim of the stack and attach it with egg whites.

12. Center the roof on top of the cabin and attach it with Royal Icing. Stick a toothpick into the bottom of the smokestack and insert the other end of the toothpick into the top of the cylinder, about ¼ inch from the front, gluing it on with Royal Icing.

13. To decorate the sides of the cabin, roll out 1 ounce of yellow gum paste to ⅛ inch thick. Cut four ⅞ x 1⅜-inch rectangles. Cut two 2½ x 1¼-inch rectangles. Allow these yellow pieces to dry for 15 minutes; this will make it easier to cut out the centers. Once they are slightly firm use a scalpel and a ruler to cut the rectangles into frames about ⅛ inch thick (see photo on page 183).

14. Roll ½ ounce of black gum paste paper thin and cut it into rectangles slightly smaller than the four window frames. Attach the pieces of black gum paste to the backs of the windows with dabs of egg whites. Let them sit until they are easy to handle (if your workspace is humid, let them sit overnight and apply them at the very end). Attach two windows and one frame to each side of the cabin with egg whites. Place the frame ½ inch above the bottom of the cabin cake, centered on the side of the cabin. Align the windows with the edges of the frame and attach them ½ inch above the frame.

15. To decorate the front end of the cylinder, roll out 4 ounces of blue fondant to 3/16 inch thick. Cut one circle using a 2½-inch round cutter and one with a 3¾-inch round cutter. Use a #6 pastry tip to emboss rivets around the edge of the smaller round, approximately ¼ inch apart.

16. Attach the smaller circle to the center of the larger circle and then attach the entire piece to the front end of the cylinder with egg whites.

17. Make the headlight by rolling ½ ounce of red gum paste out to ⅝ inch thick and using a 1-inch round cutter to cut a circle. Round the front of the circle with your fingers and press a slight indentation into the center. Roll a pea-size amount of yellow gum paste out to 1/16 inch and cut out a circle with a ¾-inch round cutter. Attach the yellow circle to the center of the red circle, in the indentation. Attach the entire piece to the center of the decorated cylinder end with egg whites.

18. Roll ¼ ounce of blue fondant out to 3/16 inch thick. Cut one ⅛ x 1½-inch strip and wrap the strip around the red headlight, against the front of the cylinder. Cut another strip of blue fondant, ⅛ x 5 inches, and wrap it around the bottom of the smokestack.

19. Use the remaining 2 ounces of blue fondant to form two side cylinders for the train. Form the fondant into two tubes that are 2 inches long, ¾ inch wide, and ¾ inch thick. Use a paring knife to square off two sides of the logs so they look like quarter-cylinders. The shape will be ¾ inch tall and wide and about 2 inches long. Use pea-size amounts of red and black gum paste, rolled paper thin, and cut four ⅛ x 1½-inch red strips and four 1/16 x 1½-inch black strips, 2 for each quarter-cylinder. Attach the strips with egg whites to the curved side of the quarter-cylinders, red stripes on the outside and black stripes toward the center (see photo on page 182). Set aside.

20. Make the smaller smokestack by rolling out ½ ounce of the yellow gum paste to ⅜ inch thick and another ½ ounce yellow gum paste to 3/16 inch thick. Use a #808 pastry tip (or a ⅝-inch round cutter) to cut one circle from each thickness. Use a ⅞-inch round cutter to cut another circle from the thinner piece of gum paste and a #10 tip to cut another circle from the thicker gum paste. Trim the #10-size circle to ¼ inch tall. Attach all the pieces of gum paste together as shown in the photo, using egg whites. Attach the stack between the cabin and the large smokestack on top of the cylinder cake with egg whites or Royal Icing.

use a scalpel or paring knife to create tiny slits that resemble fringe. Place the open loop around the knob and attach the rope to the cake and cake board with tiny amounts of water, twisting it more as needed.

25. Use white glue to attach a decorative ribbon around the cake base.

HOT TIP

* To deconstruct this cake, remove the smokestack and roof of the cab. Use a serrated knife to slice straight down, directly into the top of the cylinder and cabin cakes, until you hit the support board. Serve the entire top tier, then remove the support board and the dowels from the bottom tier. Slice and serve the bottom tier.

21. Roll out any remaining yellow gum paste to ¹⁄₁₆ inch thick and cut three skinny stripes, ⅛ x 10 inches, attaching them around the cylinder (one near the front, one 2 inches in, and one right at the front of the cabin) with egg white. Attach the two side cylinders.

22. Decorate the train further by cutting four dots with a #12 tip out of a tiny piece of red gum paste rolled out paper thin. Place the dots as shown in the photo, in the upper corners of cabin and on the front corners of the support board, and attach them with water or egg whites.

23. Form a knob on the wedge plow by rolling ¼ ounce of black gum paste into a ball. Cut out a dot from the ball with a #12 tip. Roll the leftover black into a dome and attach the dome to the dot. Attach the knob to the top center of the wedge plow.

24. Make "string" to attach to the knob by rolling 1 ounce of red gum paste into a long rope, about ¹⁄₁₆ inch wide and 24 inches long. Fold the rope in half and twist it together, keeping a small loop open at one end that you can fit around the black knob. Twist the entire piece together; using a little water as you go to help the ends stick together. When you reach the end of your rope (!),

Sock Monkey Cake

YIELD: 15 to 20 servings

Sock monkeys have become dear to me. The first sculpted sock monkey we made was over two feet tall; it was for a Food Network birthday cake competition filmed for television in Las Vegas. People saw it and loved it and started requesting it frequently for children's parties. Sock Monkeys are the quintessential old-fashioned toy for children, and adults love and often collect them too. Since our first sock monkey, we have made smaller versions, even tiny ones for cupcakes, sitting up on swirls of frosting. Our most recent sock monkey project was for another Food Network cake competition (entitled "Extreme Cakes"), and the sock monkey was over six feet tall! This cake is perfect for a newborn, a cuddly five-year-old… or the 16- (or 30-) year-old who just won't part with his favorite stuffed animal.

WHAT YOU NEED

RECIPES

1½ cake recipes (see Basic Recipes, pages 64–69) to make three 6-inch rounds, 2 inches high (or you can cut six 6-inch rounds out of sheet pans); and one 8-inch round, 2 inches high (or you can bake two 8-inch rounds that are 1 inch high)

1½ frosting recipes (see Basic Recipes, page 71–77)

1 recipe Royal Icing (page 78)

MATERIALS

2½ pounds gum paste

Shortening (for rolling out gum paste and marzipan)

Luster dust: silver

Lemon extract

Food-coloring gels: lemon yellow, royal blue, leaf green, super red, coal black, sunset orange, buckeye brown

Egg whites

5 pounds fondant (includes 2 pounds for cake base)

Cornstarch (for rolling out fondant)

Vodka (for painting wood)

12 ounces marzipan

Food-coloring powder: cocoa brown

EQUIPMENT

Scalpel

Toothpicks

Plastic mat

Small and large rolling pins

Strainer (for rolling out fondant)

One 14-inch round cake base (made from 3 layers of cardboard glued together or store-bought)

Ruler

Dry pastry brush

Fondant smoothers

Paring knife

Pastry tips: #2, #9, #12, #804, #806, #809

Round cutters: ⅞-inch, 1¼-inch; star cutter: 1-inch (optional); heart cutter: ⅝-inch (optional)

Tomato leaf template (page 214)

Stitching tool (optional)

(CONTINUED ON NEXT PAGE)

WHAT YOU NEED

EQUIPMENT (CONTINUED)

Large and small serrated knives

3 round cake cardboards: two 6-inch and one 8-inch

One 5-inch round support board (1 piece foam core or 2 pieces of cardboard glued together in advance)

Offset spatula(s)

Scissors

Pastry bag and coupler

Small rubber spatula

Twelve ¾-inch-wide plastic dowels: 7 approximately 4 inches long; 5 approximately 1 inch long

1 long wooden dowel, approximately 10 inches long and ¼ inch wide

Wooden skewers

Pen

Palette knife

Pencil sharpener

Mallet or hammer

Small paintbrush with stiff bristles

Clay gun tool with ¹⁄₁₆-inch and optional ¹⁄₃₂-inch round disc attachments

Turntable (optional)

Small paintbrushes

7-inch round plate or cardboard circle

Ball tool or dog bone tool

White glue

Decorative ribbon

TECHNIQUES

Dyeing fondant, gum paste, and marzipan (page 50)

Covering cake with fondant (page 41)

Splitting cake (page 36)

Sculpting cake (page 39)

Crumb coating cake (page 40)

Filling a pastry bag (page 26)

Filling cake (page 38)

Piecing fondant (page 44)

Doweling sculpted cakes (page 47)

Wood staining (page 51)

Deconstructing cakes (page 48)

METHOD

At least three days to one week in advance: *Make the pins and needles.*

For this cake the only sugar decorations that *need* to dry ahead of time are the pins and needles for the pincushion, and the larger needle on the cake. But if you can, make the buttons, thimble, pincushion, and strawberry ahead of time, too; this will make them easier to handle. **Be sure to create a few extra pins and needles because they are very delicate and prone to breakage.**

1. Create 1 large needle for the cake. Roll ¼ ounce of gum paste into a long, skinny string about ⅛ inch thick and 4 inches long on a smooth surface coated with shortening. Shape one end into a point (just like a real needle). On the other end, use a scalpel to create a ¼-inch slit for the eye of the needle. Use a toothpick to open the eye of the needle and smooth the edges. Allow the needle to dry straight on a flat surface for at least 3 days. Once the needle is dry,

paint it with a mixture of silver luster dust and lemon extract.

2. Create 2 smaller needles for the tomato pincushion. Form the smaller needles using the same method as above, but make them only ¹⁄₁₆ inch thick and 1¼ inch long. Allow them to dry straight on a flat surface for at least 3 days. Once the needles are dry, paint them with a mixture of silver luster dust and lemon extract.

3. Create about 16 pins. Roll gum paste into extremely thin strings that are as long as you can make them in one piece (or use a clay gun fitted with a ¹⁄₃₂-inch round opening on a disc). Cut them at different lengths, from ½ inch to 2 inches long. Remember to make a few extra in case of breakage because they are so thin. Allow them to dry straight on a flat surface for at least 3 days. Once the pins are dry, paint them with a mixture of silver luster dust and lemon extract.

4. Make the pin heads. Use about ¼ ounce of gum paste and divide it into 5 tiny pieces. Dye each piece a different color: bright yellow, lime green, sky blue, orange, and red. We have assigned each color a different size to give the pinheads variety. Roll each color into a few balls in specific sizes: ⅛ inch, ³⁄₁₆ inch, and ¼ inch. Use a toothpick to poke a hole into (but not through) each ball to accommodate the pin. Glue the pinheads to the pins by brushing a dab of egg white onto one end of the pins and push the balls on to secure them.

HOT TIP

* If you are short on time, cut and paint some cloth-covered wires to look like pins. Just make sure you don't eat them!

One day in advance: *Make the cake base.* Dye 2 pounds of fondant bright orange. Roll it out to ⅛ inch thick on a plastic mat coated with shortening and use it to cover the cake base. Let it dry overnight in a cool area.

MAKE THE REMAINING DECORATIONS

You don't *need* to make these decorations ahead of time, but if you want to get a head start you could make them up to a week in advance; giving them time to dry will make them easier to handle.

THIMBLE

1. Roll ¼ ounce of gum paste into a cylinder about 1 inch tall. The thimble should be about ⅞ inch wide at the base and ⅝ inch wide at the top.

2. Make an indentation at the top of the thimble using a #806 pastry tip and press in slightly using your finger.

3. Roll out a 2½ x ¹⁄₁₆-inch string to wrap around the base and attach it with some egg white. Use a toothpick to poke tiny indentations in an even pattern on the top and the upper sides of the thimble to give some detail.

4. Paint the thimble using a mixture of silver luster dust and lemon extract.

BUTTONS

1. You will need about 35 to 40 buttons, 8 to 10 for each color and size. Divide 4 ounces of gum paste into 4 pieces. Dye one portion yellow, one lime green, and one sky blue, keeping the last portion white. We made the different colored buttons different sizes, but all the buttons are created using the same method.

2. Work with one color at a time. Roll half of the color out to ⅛ inch thick and the other half to ¹⁄₁₆ inch thick on a plastic mat coated with shortening.

3. Cut the **outside** of the button from the ⅛-inch sheet using these tips: for white, #804; for green, #806; for yellow, #809; for blue, ⅞-inch round cutter.

4. Cut the **inside** of the button from the ¹⁄₁₆-inch sheet using these tips: for white, #12; for green, #804; for yellow, #806; for blue, #809.

5. Form all of the **outside** rounds into rings by using the pastry tip that you used to cut the inside of the button and cutting the middle out. This ring will be the outer edge of the button.

6. Using egg white, glue the thinner circles into their respective outside rings. Use a #2 pastry tip to cut thread holes into the inside circles.

TOMATO PIN CUSHION AND STRAWBERRY

1. Dye 9 ounces of gum paste tomato red, using super red, sunset orange, and a touch of buckeye brown food-coloring gels. Dye ½ ounce of gum paste dark green using leaf green, royal blue, and coal black food-coloring gels. Set the green aside.

2. Form 8 ounces of the red gum paste into a ball and shape it like a tomato (it should be about 2⅛ inches tall and 3 inches wide). Use a toothpick, the end of a scalpel, or the tip of a paring knife to crease the tomato into six

equal sections. Form the remaining 1 ounce of red gum paste into a strawberry shape (about 1½ inches long and 1⅛ inches wide at the top). Crease the top of the strawberry using a toothpick or back of a scalpel.

3. Roll the dark green gum paste out to ¹⁄₁₆ inch thick on a plastic mat coated with shortening. Use the tomato leaf template (page 214) and cut out the shape for the top of the tomato. Align the openings of the leaf with the creases in the tomato. Use a stitching tool or a toothpick to create stitching marks along the edge of the tomato leaf.

4. Create the stitching detail on the tomato by cutting six 3½ x ¹⁄₁₆-inch strips and applying them to the tomato along the creases, between the indents of the leaf. They should stick on their own, but if not, apply some egg white or water with a small brush. Use a toothpick or the end of a scalpel and make indentations every ⅛ inch to create a stitched effect.

5. From the rolled out green gum paste, cut out a star using a 1-inch star cutter (or cut it by hand if you don't have a cutter; see template page 214). Round the star tips slightly with the back of a scalpel or the side of a paring knife and place the star on top of the strawberry. Form the stitching inside the outer edge of the star using a stitching tool or toothpick, just as you did with the tomato leaf.

6. Cut another string, 1 inch long and ¾ inch wide, and form into a loop. Place it in the center on top of the tomato and attach it with a dab of egg white.

MAKE AND ASSEMBLE THE CAKE

1. Prepare the cake batter, pour into three 6-inch round pans (at least 2 inches high, or you can cut six 6-inch rounds out of half-sheets) and one 8-inch round pan (at least 2 inches high). Bake according to the recipe. Let cool for 20 minutes, remove from pans, then wrap tightly in plastic wrap and freeze for at least one hour. (This will make them easier to cut.)

2. While the cake is chilling, make the filling and Royal Icing.

3. Cut the curved tops off the round cakes and split the cakes into 1-inch layers or cut six 6-inch rounds from the sheet pans. You should have six 6-inch round layers and two 8-inch round layers, all 1 inch high.

4. Create the bottom and top of the spool. Place a small dab of filling on one 6-inch round cardboard and the 8-inch round cardboard. Place one 8-inch round layer on top of each. Sculpting each cake with a small serrated knife, shape the cake on the 6-inch round board to be the top of the spool. It should measure 8 inches wide across the top and taper to 6 inches wide on the bottom. The cake on the 8-inch round cardboard is for the bottom of the spool and should be carved so it is 6 inches wide at the top and angled out to 8 inches wide on the bottom.

Once the cakes are sculpted, cut away any excess cardboard with a serrated knife or scissors. Crumb coat the cakes with a thin layer of filling. Put them back in the refrigerator to chill while you create the center of the spool out of cake.

5. For the center spool you will need to dowel **inside** the cake. Place a dab of filling on the remaining 6-inch round cardboard. Stack and fill three 6-inch round layers of cake with two ½-inch layers of filling between. Cut four plastic dowels to the height of this tier (approximately 4 inches high). Place the dowels into the bottom tier in a circle small enough to fit underneath the 5-inch round support board. Spread a thin layer of filling on top of the dowels and lay the support board directly on top, pressing down slightly to secure it to the layers.

6. Continue to build the spool of thread. Place a dab of filling on top of the 5-inch round support board. Stack and fill (with two ½ inch layers of filling) the remaining three 6-inch round layers on top of the support board. At this point your cake should be about 8 inches high. Crumb coat the entire cake with a thin layer of filling and place in the refrigerator to chill for at least an hour while you dye and roll out the fondant. If the cake seems unstable at any time during the building or crumb coating, place it in the refrigerator to chill until it becomes sturdy.

7. Dye 8 ounces of fondant pale brown. Twist the pale brown fondant with 1 pound of white fondant for a marbleized effect. (See the wood staining technique on page 51.) Roll out half of the marbled fondant to ¼ inch thick and use it to cover the bottom-spool cake. Use the other half of the fondant to cover the top-spool cake. Set the two cakes aside.

8. To cover the center of the spool, you need to wrap fondant **around** the cake, just like wrapping a piece of paper around a bottle. Dye 1½ pounds of fondant red. Take the center of the spool out of the refrigerator and apply another thin layer of filling all over the cake. Roll out the red fondant to an 8 x 20-inch rectangle. Roll the fondant onto the rolling pin and hold the rolling pin vertically against the cake. Quickly unroll the fondant around the cake, starting in the back. Trim it and form a seam in the back. Once the cake is completely covered in the red fondant you are ready to stack the tiers and finish decorating. Remember: this layer of fondant does not have to be perfect because you are going to wrap the entire center spool again with marzipan "thread" so no one will see!

9. Before doweling, paint both the top and bottom tiers to look like wood using a paintbrush with tough bristles and a mixture of vodka and brown food-coloring gels (see page 51). Let both cakes dry for about 20 minutes.

10. Position the spool bottom slightly toward the back of the base cake and attach it with some Royal Icing. It should not be exactly centered so you'll have room for the tomato pincushion later. Cut and insert 5 plastic dowels into the center of the bottom cake. These dowels should be cut to approximately 1 inch tall. Make sure the dowels are positioned within a 6-inch circle so they fit underneath the support board for the center spool. Spread some royal icing over the dowels and attach the center spool. It should be centered directly over the dowels.

11. Cut 3 more plastic dowels to about 4 inches tall and arrange them within a 5-inch circle in the top tier of the center spool, to support the spool top. Spread some Royal Icing over the dowels, then place the spool top, centered over the spool.

12. Sharpen the end of a ¼-inch wide wooden dowel and measure the height of the cake from the base to the top tier (it should be approximately 10 inches). Cut this dowel to be slightly shorter than the entire cake. Hammer the sharpened dowel into the center of the top tier until it goes through all three tiers (the sharpened end will cut through the cake boards and support board to the bottom). The center dowel will prevent the cake from shifting. Don't worry — you will cover over this hole later when you decorate the cake.

13. Dye 12 ounces of marzipan red. Soften the marzipan by mixing in about 1 teaspoon of shortening. Push the marzipan through a clay gun fitted with a disc with a ⅛-inch-round opening to create the "thread" for the spool, which will be in segments. (Note: It is easiest to attach the "thread" if the cake is placed on a turntable so it can spin, but it's not essential.) Attach the thread one piece at a time with egg whites. Brush the egg whites on the cake, then attach the marzipan. Start at the top and continuing all around the cake until the entire spool is covered. For the last piece, attach it to the middle of the cake, coming from the back, so the spool looks as though it is unraveling.

14. Fill a pastry bag fitted with a #2 tip with Royal Icing and attach the large needle to the center of the cake. Thread a piece of marzipan through the eye of the needle and attach it with egg white.

15. If you want to decorate the top of the spool, roll out about 3 ounces of white gum paste as thin as you can (about 1/32 inch thick) on a plastic mat coated with shortening. Use a 7-inch round plate or cake board as a guide and cut out a 7-inch circle. Place the circle on top of the spool in the center. Dye 1/2 ounce of gum paste black and roll it out as thin as you can. Cut a strip that's 22 inches long and 1/8 inch wide to fit around the outside edge of the circle and attach it with some egg white. From the same piece of black dough, cut a half moon shape with a 6-inch straight edge that's 2 inches wide at the center and attach it just 1/8 inch inside of the outer edge of the white circle.

16. Now that the cake is complete, it's monkey time! You will need 1 1/4 pounds of white gum paste (or fondant or marzipan) to make the monkey. Roll 3 ounces of it into a ball and create a wide oval to form the head. Use a stitching tool or toothpick and form a stitched circle around the crown of the monkey's head, about a third of the entire head. Use another 6 ounces to form the body, rolling it into an oblong ball. Then divide 10 ounces into 5 separate portions. Roll all five of those pieces into logs about 3/4 inch wide. Create two arms that are 5 inches long. Round the ends that will be the hands and use a rolling pin to thin the other ends, which you will attach to the monkey's shoulders. Form two legs the same way but make them 1 inch

longer. Form the tail from the last log. Cut it to 3 1/2 inches long and shape one end into a point. Use a stitching tool or a toothpick to form a ring around all five appendages about one-third of the way up the arms from the end. This end will remain unpainted.

17. Roll about 1/2 ounce of gum paste into a 1-inch ball. Cut it in half and use a ball tool or dog bone tool to make indentations and form into two ears. The ears should extend about 1/2 inch from the head. Cut a toothpick in half and stick each ear onto a half of a toothpick.

18. Create a mixture of cocoa brown powdered food coloring and lemon extract and with a small, stiff-bristled paintbrush paint the entire body, the head **except** for the top crown (this should stay white), the two ears, and two-thirds of all the appendages (the one-third on the ends should remain white).

19. Start to attach the monkey to the cake by gluing the two legs to the front edge of the spool with Royal Icing. Next, place the monkey's body directly on top of the legs and glue it to the cake with Royal Icing. Drape the arms and attach them to the sides of the body, carefully attaching them at the shoulder and at the wrists (or wherever they touch the surface of the cake!) using both egg white and Royal Icing for a strong hold. Attach the head on top of the body with a dab of Royal Icing and glue on the two ears, just at the halfway point, sticking the toothpicks directly in the side of the head to help secure them.

20. Roll out 1/4 ounce of gum paste to about 1/2 inch thick and shape it into an oval about 1 1/2 inches wide to form the nose and mouth area. Use egg white and a small brush to attach this to the lower half of the monkey's face. Use a stitching tool or toothpick and create stitching marks along the border.

21. Roll out a pea-size amount of red gum paste as thin as you can (about 1/32 inch) and cut out the mouth, which should be about 1 inch wide. Attach it with egg white.

22. Roll out a pea-size amount of black gum paste as thin as you can (about 1/32 inch) and cut out two circles for the nostrils using a #2 pastry tip, two circles for the eyes using a #9 pastry tip, and two tiny slivers for the eyebrows. Attach the nostrils, eyes, and eyebrows with dabs of egg white.

23. Lastly, the monkey needs a heart! Roll out a pea-size amount of orange gum paste to 1/16 inch thick and cut out a heart using a scalpel or 5/8-inch heart cutter. Attach the heart to the monkey's upper chest and create stitching detail with a toothpick.

24. Roll a string of green gum paste, 4 inches long and 1/16 inch wide, and attach it with some egg white between the tomato and the strawberry so it connects the two.

25. Use Royal Icing to glue the tomato, strawberry, thimble, and buttons to the cake base. Use a toothpick to create indentations in the tomato and then insert the pins and needles into the pincushion.

26. Use white glue to attach a decorative ribbon around the cake base.

Monster Cake

Wat could be more fun than a cuddly, cute . . . monster! With his googly eyes and colorful party hat, he will be the center of attention at any celebration. Create an initial or number and place it on his belly or hat to personalize the cake. Making his fur does take some time, so you could eliminate that step and keep his body smooth and he will still look great.

WHAT YOU NEED

RECIPES

2½ cake recipes (see Basic Recipes, pages 64–69) to make three 6-inch rounds, 1-inch high (or you can cut three 6-inch rounds out of a sheet pan; and three 9-inch rounds, 2-inches high

2½ frosting recipes (see Basic Recipes, pages 71–77)

½ recipe Royal Icing (page 78)

MATERIALS

3 pounds gum paste

Food-coloring gels: lemon yellow, royal blue, violet, coal black, electric pink, sunset orange, leaf green, buckeye brown

8 pounds fondant

Shortening (for rolling out gum paste)

Cornstarch (for rolling out fondant)

Egg whites

EQUIPMENT

Toothpicks

Ruler

Scalpel or paring knife

Ball tool

2 small wooden dowels for arms, approximately 5 inches long and ⅛ inch wide

Plastic mat

Small and large rolling pins

One 14-inch round cake base, made from 3 layers of cardboard glued together or store-bought

Strainer (for rolling out fondant)

Dry pastry brush

Fondant smoothers

2 round cake boards, one 7-inch and one 4½-inch, made from foam core or 2 pieces of cardboard cut and glued together in advance

One 6-inch round support board, made from foam core or 2 pieces of cardboard cut and glued together in advance

Large and small serrated knives

Sharp pointed scissors

Pastry bag and coupler

Small rubber spatula

Wooden skewers

Pen

Palette knife

7 plastic dowels, approximately 4 inches long and ¾ inch wide

Pencil sharpener

1 long wooden dowel, approximately 12 inches long and ¼ inch wide

Mallet or hammer

White glue

Offset spatula(s)

6-inch round plate or cardboard

Pastry tips: #1, #804, #809

Small paintbrush

Round cutters: 1-inch, 1½-inch

Decorative ribbon

(CONTINUED ON NEXT PAGE)

WHAT YOU NEED (CONTINUED)

TECHNIQUES

Dyeing fondant and gum paste
(page 50)

Covering cake with fondant (page 41)

Splitting cake (page 36)

Filling a pastry bag (page 26)

Filling cake (page 38)

Doweling sculpted cakes (page 47)

Sculpting cake (page 39)

Crumb coating cake (page 40)

Deconstructing cakes (page 48)

METHOD

Set aside 2 ounces of white gum paste for the horns, eyes, teeth, toenails, and fingernails.

At least two days and up to one week in advance: *Make the hat and hands.*

HAT

1. Dye 1 pound of gum paste bright orange. You will only need 6 ounces for the hat; wrap the rest tightly and save it for later use. For the bright orange color we used sunset orange mixed with a touch of lemon yellow and buckeye brown.

2. Roll 6 ounces of orange gum paste into a pointed cone, approximately 2¾ inches around the base and 3¾ inches tall. Pinch the bottom edge of the hat to form a sharp edge to meet the monster's head. Curve the top of the hat slightly. Let the hat dry overnight. The next day use a paring knife to scoop out the inside of the hat so the walls of the hat are about ½ inch thick. Allow it to dry for at least 1 more day. The outside should have formed a crust but the inside

should still be soft. Removing the inside will allow the hat to dry faster and will decrease the amount of weight sitting on the monster's head. Wrap and save the inside pieces for later use. You can decorate the hat just before you place it on the cake.

HANDS

1. Dye ½ pound of gum paste fuchsia, using electric pink and violet coloring gels. Wrap and set aside 1 ounce of this color to be used later. Divide the remaining 7 ounces into 2 equal parts. Wrap one piece and set aside.

2. Roll one portion of the fuchsia gum paste into a cone, approximately 3½ inches long and 2 inches wide. Use a paring knife to cut three slits into the wide end of the cone to form four individual fingers. Use a little shortening on your fingertips to smooth the edges, rounding the individual fingers to different sizes. Round the smaller end of the cone into a wrist.

3. Repeat to make the second hand.

4. Use the small end of a ball tool to make an indentation at the end of each finger to hold the fingernails. Use an ⅛-inch-wide wooden dowel to make a hole from the wrist to the center of the hand. Remove the dowel. Repeat the method for the other hand and allow the hands to dry for at least 2 days.

At least one day in advance: *Make the cake base.*
Dye 2 pounds of fondant bright yellow. Roll it out to ⅛ inch thick on a plastic mat coated with shortening and cover the cake base. Let dry overnight in a cool area.

MAKE THE WHITE
SUGAR DECORATIONS

Use the 2 ounces of white gum paste you set aside and coat your palms with a bit of shortening to help you create the shapes described below. These decorations do not *need* to be made ahead of time, but it is best if they dry at least overnight. That will make them easier to handle and attach to the cake.

HORNS

Divide ½ ounce of gum paste into two equal portions. Roll both portions into pointed cones about 2¼ inches long and ⅝ inch wide at the base. Curve slightly and let dry.

EYEBALLS

Roll ¾ ounce of gum paste into a ball and cut it into two equal portions. Reshape the pieces slightly so they are round on one side and flat on the other, and approximately 1 inch wide and ⅝ inch tall.

TEETH

On a smooth surface, roll ¼ ounce of gum paste into a skinny log about ¼ inch wide. Divide the log into 12 pieces, each about the size of a pea but not exactly the same size as each other. Roll the pieces into pointed cones of random widths and lengths, from ½ inch long to 1 inch long. Flatten the top of each wider end so you can attach them easily to the mouth.

TOENAILS

Divide ¼ ounce of gum paste into 8 randomly sized balls. Roll the balls into pointed cones of varying length, keeping the wide ends approximately ⅛ inch to ¼ inch wide. Slightly curve the nails and allow them to dry.

Divide ¼ ounce of gum paste into 8 balls. Roll the balls into pointed cones roughly ⅞ inch long. Keep the widest ends about ⅛ inch wide. Slightly curve the nails and allow them to dry.

MAKE AND ASSEMBLE THE CAKE

1. Prepare the cake batter, pour into three 6-inch round pans, at least 1 inch high (or sheet pans) and three 9-inch round pans, at least 2 inches high. Bake according to the recipe. Let the cakes cool for 20 minutes and remove from the pans. Wrap tightly in plastic wrap and freeze for at least one hour. This will make the cakes easier to cut.

2. While the cake is chilling, make the filling and Royal Icing.

3. Cut off the tops of the round cakes and split the cakes into 1-inch cake layers. You should have 3 layers of 6-inch rounds and 6 layers of 9-inch rounds.

4. Create the bottom tier of cake, which is the monster's body. The tiers will be internal, and you will be doweling **inside** the cake (see illustration on page 196). Place a small dab of filling on the 7-inch round cake board. Stack and fill (with two ½-inch layers of filling) three 9-inch layers of round cake. When the top layer of cake is on, push down slightly to secure the layers. Cut 4 plastic dowels to the height of this tier (approximately 3¾ inches). Insert the dowels into the bottom tier in the shape of a square that will fit underneath the 6-inch support board. Spread a thin layer of filling on top of the dowels and place the support board directly on top. Press down slightly to attach it to the bottom tier. Continue to build the body of the monster. Place a dab of filling on top of the support board. Stack and fill (with ½-inch layers of filling) the remaining three 9-inch round layers on top of the support board. At this point your cake should be about 8 inches high. Place in the refrigerator to chill for at least 1 hour while you build the head.

5. Build the head using the three 6-inch layers of cake. Place a dab of filling on the 4½-inch round cake board. Stack and fill the 3 layers of cake with two ½-inch layers of filling. When the top layer is on, press gently to secure the layers. The head should be about 4 inches high. Place the head in the refrigerator and chill for at least one hour until it is firm. Chilling makes the cakes easier to carve.

6. Using large and small serrated knives, carve the head and body into the shapes needed for the monster. Sculpt the head into an almost perfect ball with a flat bottom. The head should be 5½ inches wide across the middle and 4½ inches wide at the neck. The head should remain 4 inches high. Round the body on all sides, carving it to 7 inches wide at the base, 8½ inches wide across the middle (this is the widest point), and 4½ inches wide at the neck. The body should remain 8 inches high.

them look like fur. Attach 3 tufts of fur to each foot, between the toes and the body, in a row, using egg white. Squeeze the tufts together so there is no space between the pieces, and trim excess with a knife. Fluff the fur as before. The fur should cover the joint between the feet and the body.

22. Attach the hands. Cut the two ⅛-inch wooden dowels to about 5 inches long and insert them into the hands to make sure the holes you made earlier did not close during drying. Remove the dowels from the hands. Next, create the fur that will surround the wrists. Divide 4 ounces of the orange gum paste into four 1-ounce balls. Form each ball into a cone and cut the thicker ends of the cones with sharp scissors, as before, to make the fur. Slide the dowel for the hand through the centers of the fur tufts to make holes. Then remove the dowel from the fur and insert it about 2 inches into the cake, roughly 7 inches up from the bottom of the monster, at an angle so the hand will point upward when attached. Slide two fur tufts per side onto the dowel and attach them to the side of the cake using egg whites. Fill the ring between the fur and the dowel with Royal Icing and add icing to the hole inside the hand. Apply egg white inside the fur and around the dowels. Press the hands onto the dowels and into the fur. Fluff the fur around the wrist. Repeat with the other hand. Use the pastry bag filled with Royal Icing and fitted with a #1 tip to attach the fingernails.

23. Use the remaining 4 ounces of orange gum paste to form the tail. Roll the gum paste into a chubby cone about 12 inches long and 1¾ inches thick at its widest point. With a rolling pin, press down the thick end until it is thin enough to fit under the monster's body. You should flatten the tail starting about 2½ inches from the end.

24. Roll out all the remaining fuchsia gum paste (about 1 ounce) to paper thin on a plastic mat coated with shortening. Cut it into 5 stripes about 1 inch wide and 4 inches long, plus one stripe that's 8½ inches long. Wrap 4 of the 4-inch stripes around the tail. Space them about 1¼ inches apart and attach them with egg white or water. Join the ends underneath the tail and trim to make an even seam. Attach the tail to the cake base and to the back of the monster, positioned so it curves slightly away from the body, using egg white or Royal Icing.

25. Wrap the remaining 4-inch stripe and the 8½-inch stripe around the hat. Brush the entire hat with egg whites. Wrap the longer strip around the bottom of the hat on a diagonal. Then wrap the other strip around the hat approximately 1 inch above the first strip. Trim the ends of the strips where they meet with a paring knife or scalpel to form smooth seams.

26. Attach the hat on top of the monster's head with Royal Icing and a toothpick for support. Attach both horns, one on either side of the hat, with Royal Icing. If they have trouble staying attached, use toothpicks.

27. For the fur around the horns you will need 2 ounces of green gum paste (1 ounce per horn). For each horn, divide 1 ounce of green gum paste into 2 portions. Roll each portion into a log and flatten with a rolling pin. Use a sharp pair of scissors to cut into fringe. Layer the fringe pieces together, gluing them with egg whites to create the tuft (see photo on page 195). Apply to the side of each horn and fluff. Repeat on other side of head.

28. To add the tassel to the hat, form ¼ ounce of royal blue gum paste into a cone and cut the wide end of the cone with scissors to form the tassel. Use the ball tool to create an indentation on the pointed side of the cone and attach the indentation to the party hat with egg whites.

29. Use white glue to attach a decorative ribbon around the cake base.

Backpack Cake

This is the perfect cake for a fall birthday, a back to school party, or any kid who is really attached to a certain backpack. We first made a cake like this for a little girl who was known by everyone in her neighborhood for her special knapsack. All the kids at her birthday party loved it! My little niece, Ruthie, loves frogs, so we put a frog patch on the big pocket. But as with any cake design, feel free to make this your own. Try a dog's face, a big heart, a butterfly, initials, or anything else the recipient might love. We completed the bag by placing it on a cake base that we decorated to look like a pad of paper with a sugar pencil — which is optional, of course, but it makes the presentation so much fun.

WHAT YOU NEED

RECIPES

3 cake recipes (see Basic Recipes, pages 64–69) to make three half-sheet cakes, 1 inch high

2 frosting recipes (see Basic Recipes, pages 71–77)

MATERIALS

2 pounds gum paste

Food-coloring gels: lemon yellow, buckeye brown, violet, super red, leaf green, sunset orange, coal black, baker's rose

Shortening (for rolling out gum paste)

Egg whites

Lemon extract

Luster dust: silver

12 pounds fondant

Cornstarch (for rolling out fondant)

Vodka

EQUIPMENT

Toothpicks

Plastic mat

Small and large rolling pins

Ruler

Paring knife

Small paint brushes

Scalpel

One 16 x 11-inch cake base (made from 3 layers of cardboard)

Strainer (for rolling out fondant)

Dry pastry brush

Fondant smoothers

Red and turquoise colored pencils (optional, for cake base)

Two 9 x 5½-inch pieces of cardboard for the cake base, glued together in advance

Scissors

Pastry bag

Small rubber spatula

Pastry tips: #6, #804, #806

5 plastic dowels, approximately 5¾ inches tall and ¾ inch wide

One 6 x 4-inch rectangle support board (1 piece foam core or 2 pieces of cardboard glued together in advance)

Large and small serrated knives

Offset spatula(s)

Stitching tool

Veining tool (optional)

Template for frog head (page 214)

Round cutters: 1-inch, 1¼-inch

Clay gun tool with ⅛-inch round disc attachment

White glue

(CONTINUED ON NEXT PAGE)

METHOD

***At least three days and up to one week in
advance:*** *Make the decorations and cake
base (optional).*

PENCIL

1. To make a standard-size pencil to
   decorate the cake base, dye ½ ounce
   of gum paste light brown, ¼ ounce
   pencil yellow, and a pea-size amount
   pink (for the eraser).

2. On a plastic mat lightly coated with
   shortening, roll the light brown gum
   paste into a tube ¼ inch thick and
   5½ inches long. Form one end into a
   point that begins tapering about
   ¾ inch from the end and cut the
   other end flat, using a paring knife.

3. Roll out the yellow gum paste as thin
   as possible. Cut a 5 x ½-inch strip.
   Brush one side of the strip with a thin
   coat of egg white and wrap it around
   the pencil. Trim the gum paste into a
   straight seam where it comes together.
   (This will be on the bottom so no one
   will see.) At the flat end of the pencil,

trim the yellow gum paste ¼ inch from
the end. At the pointed end, trim the
yellow gum paste where the point of the
pencil begins to taper. Using a scalpel
or paring knife, cut a ragged edge at
the point end of the yellow gum paste,
with a series of narrow V shapes, to
make it look like a sharpened pencil.

4. Form the eraser. Roll the pink gum paste
   into a tube about ¾ inch long and
   ¼ inch thick. Use a scalpel to cut
   small indentations in one end of the
   tube to make it look like a used eraser.
   Cut the other end flat and glue the flat
   end to the flat end of the pencil, using a
   dab of egg whites applied with a small
   paintbrush.

5. Use a pea-size amount of any extra gum
   paste you have to make the metal
   collar. (It can be any color because you
   will paint it later.) Roll the gum paste
   out paper thin and cut a ½ x 1¼-inch
   piece. Use the back of a scalpel to
   make vertical and horizontal lines in
   the gum paste to resemble the metal
   collar on a real pencil. Use a mixture
   of silver luster dust and lemon
   extract to paint the entire piece.

6. Apply a dab of egg white with a small
   brush to the end of the pencil just
   beneath the eraser and wrap the silver
   piece around the pencil, aligning it
   with the edge of the yellow gum paste
   and overlapping the eraser. Trim any
   excess and create a straight seam
   that lines up with the seam in the
   back of the pencil. Paint the point of
   the pencil using a touch of black
   food-coloring gel and paint any
   special number or symbol near the
   eraser end of the pencil.

HOT TIP

* As you are creating the pencil, use a real
  pencil as an example to work from.
  Looking at the real object helps get all the
  details just right!

CAKE BASE

1. Roll 2 pounds of white fondant out to
   ⅛ inch thick and cover the cake base.

2. Use the back of a paring knife to
   emboss horizontal lines as close
   together as possible into three of the
   side edges of the cake (the two longer
   sides and one of the short sides) base
   so it resembles a pad of paper. Let dry
   overnight.

3. The next day, use a sharp turquoise
   colored pencil to make the horizontal
   lines on top of the cake base, on the
   bottom 3 inches of the pad of paper.
   (You only need lines on the bottom
   3 inches because the rest will be
   covered by another sheet of fondant.)
   Space the lines ½ inch apart, starting
   at the bottom of the pad.

4. Use a sharp red colored pencil to
   draw two vertical lines on the left
   side of the top of the cake base, to
   resemble notebook paper. Again, you
   only need lines on the bottom
   3 inches because the rest will be
   covered by another sheet of fondant.
   The first line should be 1½ inches
   from the left edge and the next
   should be ⅛ inch in from that.

5. Roll another 1 pound of white fondant
   out to ⅛ inch thick and cut a rectangle
   the same size as your cake base
   (about 11¼ x 16¼ inches). Allow it to
   dry for 5 minutes so it is easier to
   handle. This will be the top sheet on
   the pad of paper. If you are a detail

nut like I am, turn this piece of fondant over and draw in the turquoise and red lines on the bottom 3 inches of the page, as you did on the top of the cake base. Then flip it back over so it is right side up.

6. Use the turquoise pencil to draw horizontal stripes on the front side of this fondant sheet as you did on top of the cake base, but this time you'll need lines from top to bottom, except for the 2½-inch margin at the top. Use the red pencil to draw vertical lines as you did on the top of the cake base, going all the way from top to bottom this time.

7. Brush the top of the cake base with a thin layer of water but do not brush water over any of the lines.

8. Lay the top sheet of fondant on the cake base and adjust it so the edges are lined up evenly. Curl up the bottom corners, one more than the other, and support them with rolled up paper towels or plastic wrap. Let dry overnight in a cool area.

9. Finish the base by continuing the turquoise and red stripes onto the sides of the cake base to make it look like a full pad of paper.

10. Dye 1 ounce of gum paste brown for the binding at the top of the pad of paper. Roll the gum paste paper thin and cut a strip 11¼ inches long and 2¼ inches wide. Attach the strip to the top of the notepad with a bit of water, leaving a 1¼-inch space between the top turquoise line and the binding. Drape it to cover the end of the "pad," but leave the sides open. Trim the brown gum paste so it's flush with the edge of the cake base.

MAKE AND ASSEMBLE THE CAKE

1. Prepare the cake batter and bake in 3 half-sheet pans as directed in the recipe. Let the cakes cool for 20 minutes, remove from pans, then wrap tightly in plastic wrap and freeze for at least one hour. (This makes the cakes easier to cut.)

2. While the cake is chilling, make the filling.

3. Cut eight 9 x 5½-inch pieces of cake from the 3 half-sheets. From two of the sheets you will cut three pieces, and from the third sheet you'll only need to cut two pieces. All pieces should be 1 inch high.

4. For the backpack you will need to dowel **inside** the cake. Place a dab of filling on the 9 x 5½-inch cake base. Place the first layer of cake on the cardboard, coat it with a ½-inch layer of filling, then stack and fill 3 more cake layers with ½-inch layers of filling between them. When the top layer of cake is on, press down slightly to secure the layers. This tier should have 4 layers of cake and 3 layers of filling.

5. Cut five plastic dowels to the height of this tier (approximately 5¾ inches). Insert the dowels into the tier in an arrangement that will fit underneath the 6 x 4-inch support board. Spread

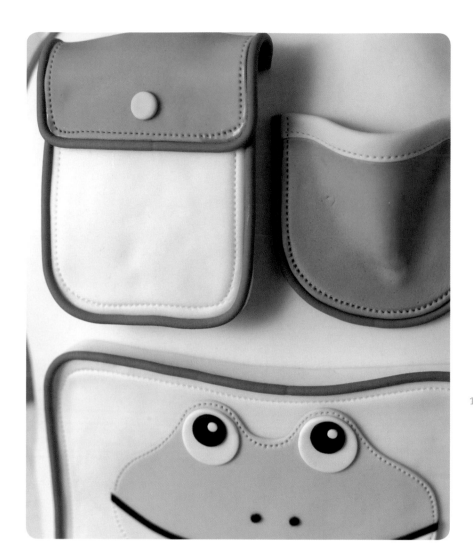

a thin layer of filling on top of the dowels and lay the support board directly on top of that, pressing down slightly to secure it.

6. Continue to build the backpack by placing a dab of filling on top of the support board. Stack and fill the 4 remaining 9 x 5½-inch cake layers with three ½-inch layers of filling, directly on top of the support board. When the top layer of cake is on, press down slightly to secure the layers. At this point your cake should be about 12 inches high.

7. Use serrated knives to sculpt the backpack. The top of the backpack

should have a rounded shape and a slight slope to the front. The back of the cake should be straight down. Give the entire backpack some "motion" by carving the corners so they are rounded and creating a few indentations along the sides. When you are finished carving, the total height should be about 11¼ inches high. The top of the bag should be 6 inches wide and 3¼ inches deep and the bottom of the bag should be 8¾ inches wide and 5½ inches deep. Use a serrated knife or scissors to cut away any excess cardboard from the bottom of the cake. Don't be afraid to cut the board

a little beneath the cake so it takes on the shape of the bottom layer.

8. Crumb coat the entire cake with a thin layer of filling and place in the refrigerator to chill for at least an hour while you mix the colors and roll out the fondant. If the cake becomes unstable at any time during the building, sculpting, or crumb coating, place in the refrigerator to chill until it becomes sturdy.

9. Dye 5 pounds of fondant butter yellow. Set aside and wrap 1⅜ pound to use later.

10. To cover the backpack, use the technique for piecing fondant (see page 44). Start with the sides of the backpack. Roll out about 2 pounds of the butter yellow fondant to ⅛ inch thick. Use a paring knife to cut two 4 x 16-inch strips. Attach the strips to the sides of the cake, lining up the edges of each strip with the back of the bag and smoothing the edge with your fingers. Overlap the strips by ¼ inch on top of the bag in the center. Use a paring knife or scalpel to cut away any excess and trim the seam to make it straight. Smooth the seam with your finger. Use the stitching tool to make a line down the center of the seam. Trim the ends of the strips of fondant at the bottom of the bag, pushing them underneath the sides of the bag with the paring knife. Keep any extra scraps of the butter yellow color to reuse.

11. Combine the scraps of butter yellow fondant with 1½ pounds of the butter yellow fondant. (You should still have 1⅜ pounds wrapped and set aside for later.) Roll out a large piece to ¼ inch

thick and cut out a rectangle about 12 inches long and 14 inches wide for the front of the cake. Use a paring knife to cut the rolled out fondant into a domed shape by cutting off the top corners and rounding the top. Use a small paintbrush to apply egg white to the front edge of the side strips, then place the dome-shape fondant on the front of the bag by rolling it up on the rolling pin. Then start at the top of the cake and unroll the fondant, letting it stick to the crumb coat. Once the fondant is on the cake, smooth it onto the front of the bag and press together the top edge of the fondant and the edge of the side strips, where you applied the egg white. Be sure the egg white glues the pieces together. Trim the bottom of the front piece of fondant. Use the stitching tool to create a line of stitching about ⅛ inch from the seam on all edges.

12. Dye another 3 pounds of fondant purple for the back of the backpack. Because there is usually more padding in the back of school bags, roll out the purple fondant to ½ inch thick. It will still stretch and become somewhat thinner. Cut it to about 12 inches tall and 8 inches wide and curve the top corners slightly to mimic the shape of the bag. Use your rolling pin to taper the edges of this piece of fondant so the outside edge is about ⅛ inch thick, beginning the slope about 1 inch from the outside edge.

13. Apply egg white to the back edges of the yellow side strips and attach the purple fondant to the back of the cake. Line up the top and sides of the purple dough with the yellow edges. Use your

fingers to press the edges together to form a smooth seam. Trim any excess fondant at the bottom of the cake, again pushing it under the cake to form the shape of the bag.

14. Use the stitching tool to make stitching lines on both sides of the seam, ⅛ inch from the edge. Make two indentations on the back of the bag using a veining tool, and then go over the indentations with the stitching tool. Use your fingers to smooth and round the edges slightly; this will make the purple fondant look even more like padding.

15. To make the straps, dye 1 pound of gum paste the same color purple as the fondant. (Note: These straps will probably not taste great — large gum paste objects usually don't — but gum paste is the strongest material to use for this and renders a look remarkably similar to fabric. It also allows you to make much thinner straps. You do not need to serve pieces of the strap when you cut the cake!)

16. To form the straps, roll the gum paste out to ⅛ inch thick. Cut two 12 x 2-inch strips. Smooth the edges using your fingers (coated with a little bit of shortening). Stretch the bottom ends of the straps, using your fingers, so they are 1½ inches wider than the top. Use a stitching tool to make stitching lines along the sides and up the center of each strap. Make the stitch marks deeper in the center to create a padded look (see photo page 209).

17. Use a brush to apply egg white to the back of each strap and attach both straps (one at a time) to the back of the bag. The tops of the straps should

be slightly off center and the bottoms should attach to the lower corners. Line up the top of a strap where the purple fondant meets the yellow, press gently to attach it, and then continue pressing the strap along the back of the pack. Leave spaces so the strap is not flat against the back of the bag. The straps should not be perfectly straight; they should look like real straps that can move. Once both straps are attached, use the stitching tool to create two lines of stitching at the top of each strap.

18. Use the reserved 1⅜ pounds of butter yellow fondant to form the pockets. Start by rolling out 1 pound on a smooth surface coated with shortening to ½ inch thick and cut out the large pocket shape: a 7 x 5-inch rectangle with corners and edges rounded and smoothed to look like fabric. Use egg white to attach the pocket to the front of the bag, about ½ inch up from the bottom. Use the stitching tool to make a line of stitching on the front of pocket, about ¼ inch from the outside edge.

19. Roll the remaining 6 ounces of yellow fondant out to ½ inch thick to form the flap pocket for the upper left corner of the backpack. Cut out a pocket shape about 4 inches tall and 3 inches wide. Smooth and round the edges and corners and attach the pocket with egg white.

20. To make the flap for the pocket you just attached, dye another 6 ounces of fondant (or gum paste) leaf green. Roll 2 ounces of it out to ⅛ inch thick and cut out the shape of the flap, which should be about 2½ inches tall and 3 inches wide. Smooth the edges

with your fingers and attach the flap to the top back of the pocket with egg white. Curve it over the front of the pocket so it looks like a real flap.

21. Dye 1½ ounces of gum paste lime green, ½ ounce black, 1 ounce purple, and 2 ounces orange. Wrap in plastic wrap and set aside.

22. To form the smallest pocket, roll out the remaining 4 ounces of leaf green fondant to ½ inch thick. Cut out a pocket that is 2¾ inches tall and 3 inches wide and smooth the edges with your fingers. Roll out a pea-size amount of the lime green gum paste into a strip 2¾ inches long and ½ inch wide and fold it over the top straight edge of the pocket shape you just cut. Use the stitching tool to create a line of stitching along the bottom edge of the lime green strip and along the sides and bottom of the pocket. Attach the pocket to the backpack with egg white, leaving the top edge unglued so you can pull the pocket open slightly.

23. Roll the remaining lime green gum paste out to 1/16 inch thick. Use a #804 pastry tip to cut out a button for the top left pocket flap. Attach the button with a dab of egg white.

24. To make the frog patch, roll out about 1 ounce of lime green gum paste to 1/16 inch thick. Cut out the shape of a frog's head using the frog head template (page 214). The head should be about 5½ inches wide and 4 inches tall. Roll out about 1 ounce of white gum paste as thin as possible and cut out the bottom part of the frog's mouth using the same template. Attach the mouth using dabs of egg

white or water. Use the 1-inch round cutter to cut out two eyes. Attach them to the frog inside the rounded area on top of his head.

25. Roll out ½ ounce of black gum paste to 1/16 inch thick. Cut two irises for the frog's eyes using a #806 pastry tip. Attach them to the white eyes, slightly off center. Cut out two white dots using a #6 pastry tip and attach them to the irises.

26. Cut a strip about 5½ inches long and ⅛ inch wide out of the black gum paste to make the smile line of the mouth. Attach the strip along the edge where the white gum paste meets the green. Use a stitching tool to make stitching marks down the center of the black line. Make stitching marks all along the outside edge of the frog, about ⅛ inch from the edge. Cut out two nostrils from the black gum paste using a #6 pastry tip and attach them to the frog above the center of the mouth using a tiny dab of egg white or water.

HOT TIP

* When attaching fondant or gum paste that has been dyed a dark saturated color (e.g., black, dark purple, green, red), use liquid (such as water or egg white) sparingly or the color will bleed.

27. To make the backpack's zipper, roll 1 ounce of purple fondant as thin as possible. Cut a long strip, about 17½ inches long and 1¼ inches wide. Use a scalpel or paring knife to score

a narrow rectangle in the center of the strip, about ¼ inch wide and 17 inches long (the ends of the rectangle should be about ½ inch from the ends of the strip). This is the outline for the zipper. Center the strip on top of the bag and attach it with egg white. Use the stitching tool to make lines of stitching along the outer edge of the strip and around the center of the scored rectangle. Use a scalpel or X-acto knife to make the zipper teeth. Score horizontal lines all along the rectangle about 1/16 inch apart, leaving more space (about ⅛ inch) between them at the ends. Then score alternating vertical lines between the horizontal lines, but don't add vertical lines to the wider spaces at the ends of the zipper.

28. Use a mixture of silver luster dust and lemon extract to paint the zipper teeth silver, using a small paintbrush.

29. Make the base of the zipper from about ¼ ounce of leftover gum paste (you can use any color because you will paint it silver later). Roll it into a ½-inch ball. Flatten the ball slightly and shape it into a zipper pull (use a real zipper as a guide). It should be about ½ inch long, and about ⅜ inch wide and rounded on one side, and about ¼ inch wide and straight on the other (see illustration A). Next, roll out a strip about ⅛ inch wide and ½ inch long for the center of the zipper. Curve it and glue the two ends of the strip on top of the zipper, leaving the center open (insert a small piece of rolled up plastic wrap to hold its shape until it stiffens slightly) so the zipper pull can fit inside (see illustration B).

30. Make a horseshoe-shaped ring by rolling a thin tube of gum paste, about ¹⁄₁₆ inch thick and 1 inch long. Use egg white to attach the ring to the curved opening on top of the zipper base (see illustration C). Roll out a tiny pea-size amount of gum paste paper thin, and cut another strip, about ⅛ inch wide and ½ inch long. Wrap one end of this piece around the ring (see illustration D). Paint all these pieces silver.

31. Shape a pea-size amount of gum paste into an oval about ¾ inch long and ¼ inch wide. Paint it black with a mixture of vodka and black food coloring. Let it dry for 10 minutes, then attach to the end of the zipper pull with egg white.

32. Roll out the remaining lime green gum paste paper thin and cut a 1¼-inch circle with a round cutter. Cut the circle in half and make stitching marks along the edges. Attach each half-circle to the ends of the purple zipper strip with egg white.

33. To create the orange piping around the backpack, it's easiest to use a clay gun fitted with a ⅛-inch round disc. Soften 1 ounce of orange gum paste with about ½ teaspoon of shortening and feed through the clay gun to press out long strings. For the outer seams on the front and back of the backpack you will need two 30-inch-long strings. For the outside edge of the largest pocket, form one 24-inch string (when you attach it, make sure that the ends of the string meet in the center of the bottom of the pocket). Press out an 8-inch string for the edge of the smallest green pocket. Press out two 10-inch strings to fit around

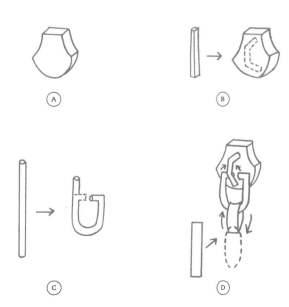

the top flap and the bottom of the pocket for the pocket in the upper left corner of the backpack. Attach the strings along the seams of the backpack (see photo opposite), using a small brush to apply egg white.

34. Apply nontoxic white glue to the cake base and place the backpack on the base, a little off-center, being careful not to knock into the raised edges on the pad of paper. (Remember, there is cardboard under the bottom of the cake so the cake will never touch glue!)

35. For the loop on the top of the back-pack, roll out the remaining 1 ounce of orange gum paste and to ⅛ inch thick. Cut a strip that's 1 inch wide and 8 inches long. Use a paring knife to score intersecting diagonal lines all over the surface of the strip, on both sides, to create a webbed texture. Form a loop at the top of the bag by folding the ends of the strip forward. Attach the loop to the top of the bag with egg white. Line up the ends on top of the orange piping and in the center of the backpack straps. Trim any excess and prop up the loop with rolled up paper towels or plastic wrap until it dries, overnight if possible.

36. Cut two more orange strips, about 1 inch wide and 3 inches long, and apply webbed texture to them as you did for the loop. Attach them with dabs of egg white underneath the shoulder straps along the cake base. Prop them up slightly with paper towels or plastic wrap until they dry.

37. If you made the pencil, attach it to the cake base with egg white. On the cake base pictured here we wrote a message using an actual pencil. It's okay to do that because no one will be eating the cake base!

HOT TIPS

* It is much easier to decorate this cake if it doesn't have a center dowel, so you do not have to place the cake on its base until it is almost all decorated. But if you are traveling a long distance with the cake it is a good idea to hammer in one long, sharpened wooden dowel (¼ inch wide and approximately 11 inches long) down into the center of the cake. If you plan to do this, I suggest doing so **before** you decorate the zipper.

* To deconstruct this cake, use a knife to slice straight down, directly into the top of the cake, until you hit the support board. Serve the entire top tier then remove the support board and five dowels from the next tier. Slice that tier and serve.

Cake Templates

PHOTOCOPY THESE TEMPLATES AT 150% TO HELP WITH YOUR OUTLINES.

CANDY FACTORY CAKE
(PAGE 165)

DESIRED LETTER SIZE: 2" x 3"

Cake Templates

PHOTOCOPY THIS TEMPLATE AT 245% TO HELP WITH YOUR OUTLINES.

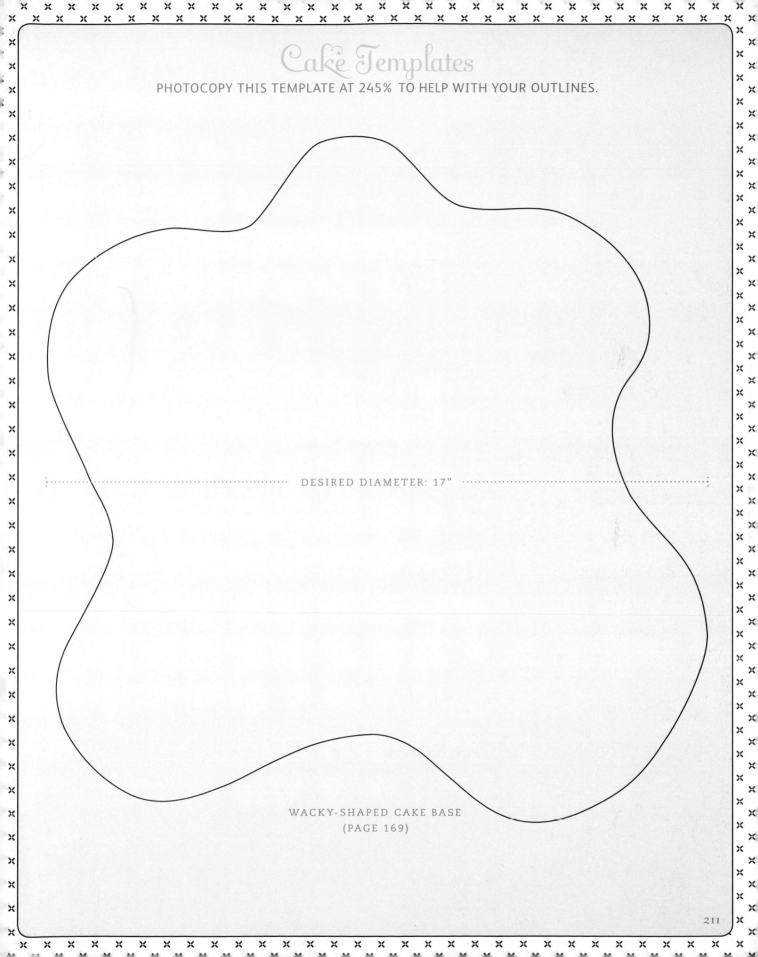

DESIRED DIAMETER: 17"

WACKY-SHAPED CAKE BASE

(PAGE 169)

DESIRED LENGTH: 12½"

QUINCEAÑERA CAKE
(PAGE 171)

Cake Templates

PHOTOCOPY THIS TEMPLATE AT 264% TO HELP WITH YOUR OUTLINES.

DESIRED DIAMETER: 18"

PETAL-SHAPED CAKE BASE

(PAGE 172)

Cake Templates

PHOTOCOPY THESE TEMPLATES TO HELP WITH YOUR OUTLINES.

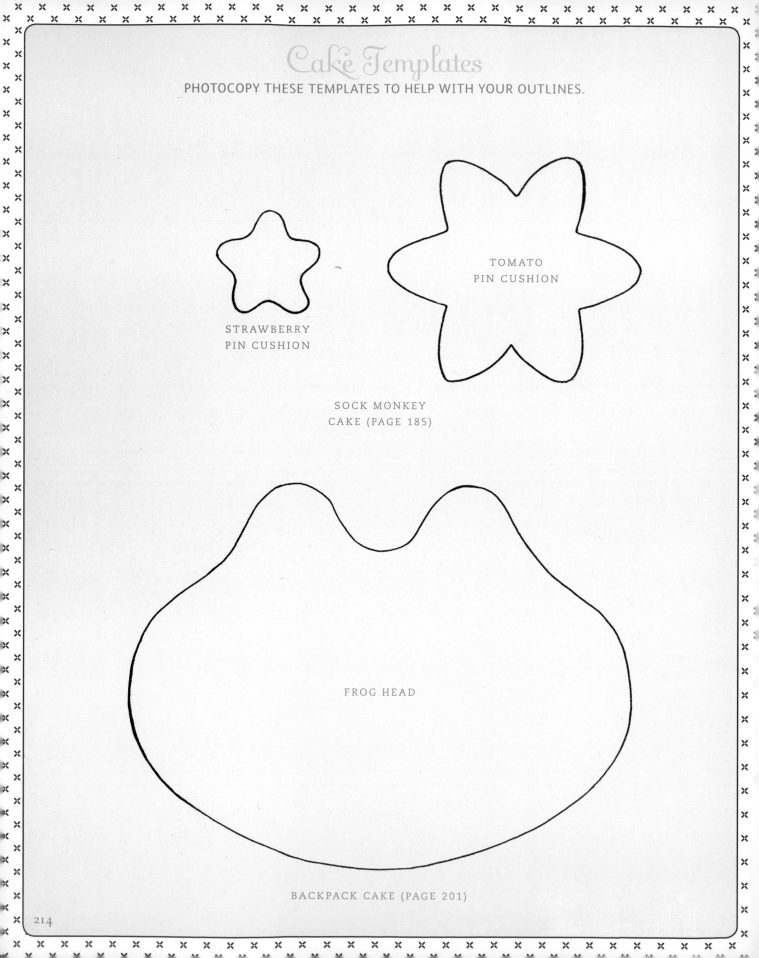

STRAWBERRY
PIN CUSHION

TOMATO
PIN CUSHION

SOCK MONKEY
CAKE (PAGE 185)

FROG HEAD

BACKPACK CAKE (PAGE 201)

Conversion Tables

LIQUID CONVERSIONS

3 teaspoons	=	1 tablespoon
1 tablespoon	=	½ ounce
2 tablespoons	=	1 ounce
¼ cup	=	2 ounces
⅓ cup	=	2¾ ounces
½ cup	=	4 ounces
¾ cup	=	6 ounces
1 cup	=	8 ounces
16 tablespoons	=	1 cup
2 cups	=	1 pint
1 pint	=	16 ounces
2 pints	=	1 quart
1 quart	=	32 ounces

WEIGHT CONVERSIONS

4 ounces	=	¼ pound
8 ounces	=	½ pound
12 ounces	=	¾ pound
16 ounces	=	1 pound
20 ounces	=	1¼ pounds
24 ounces	=	1½ pounds
28 ounces	=	1¾ pounds
32 ounces	=	2 pounds

Resources

Bakeware and Kitchen Equipment

(Many of these outlets also carry cake decorating supplies.)

BRIDGE KITCHENWARE
www.bridgekitchenware.com
711 3rd Avenue
New York, NY 10017
Phone: 212-688-4220

BROADWAY PANHANDLER
www.broadwaypanhandler.com
65 East 8th Street
New York, NY 10003
Phone: 866-966-3434

J.B. PRINCE COMPANY
www.jbprince.com
36 East 31st Street
New York, NY 10016
Phone: 800-473-0577

**KEREKES BAKERY &
RESTAURANT EQUIPMENT**
www.BakeDeco.com
6103 15th Avenue
Brooklyn, NY 11219
Phone: 800-525-5556

SUR LA TABLE
www.surlatable.com
Locations throughout the United States
Phone: 800-243-0852

WILLIAM SONOMA
www.williams-sonoma.com
Locations throughout the United States
Phone: 877-812-6235

Decorating Supplies

**BERYL'S CAKE DECORATING &
PASTRY SUPPLIES**
www.beryls.com
P.O. Box 1584
North Springfield, VA 22151
Phone: 800-488-2749

COPPERGIFTS.COM
www.coppergifts.com
Phone: 620-421-0654

CREATIVE CUTTERS
www.creativecutters.com
2495 Maine Street
Suite 410
Buffalo, NY 14214
Phone: 888-805-3444

GLOBAL SUGAR ART
www.globalsugarart.com
Phone: 800-420-6088

KITCHEN COLLECTABLES
www.kitchengifts.com
8901 J Street, Suite 2
Omaha, NE 68127
Phone: 888-593-2436

NEW YORK CAKE SUPPLIES
www.nycake.com
56 West 22nd Street
New York, NY 10010
Phone: 800-942-2539

PFEIL & HOLING
www.cakedeco.com
58-15 Northern Boulevard
Woodside, NY 11377
Phone: 800-247-7955

SUGAR WAND ENTERPRISES
www.cakesbydesign.cc
Phone: 212-362-5374
Scott Clark Woolley, owner/instructor

SUGARCRAFT
www.sugarcraft.com
2715 Dixie Hwy.
Hamilton, OH 45015
Phone: 513-896-7089

WILTON INDUSTRIES
www.wilton.com
2240 West 75th Street
Woodridge, IL 60517
Phone: 800-794-5866

Nonedible Supplies

THE CRAFT PLACE
www.thecraftplace.com
(Web orders only for Styrofoam and craft supplies)

**MICHAELS, THE ART
AND CRAFT STORE**
www.michaels.com
Locations throughout the United States
Phone: 800-MICHAELS

PAPER MART
www.papermart.com
5361 Alexander Street
Los Angeles, CA 90040
Phone: 800-745-8800

PEARL
www.pearlpaint.com
Locations throughout the United States
Phone: 800-451-7327

General Decorating Information

**INTERNATIONAL CAKE
EXPLORATION SOCIETE (ICES)**
www.ices.org
Phone: 318-746-2812

Acknowledgements

Writing any book is an enormous undertaking, but I am convinced that writing a cookbook is an even bigger challenge. Besides the words, there are so many people who help to edit, photograph, illustrate, edit, recipe-test, organize equipment, edit, fact-check, and so much more! And did I mention edit?

First and foremost, I have to thank the hundreds of people who have called and written to tell us how much they loved *The Confetti Cakes Cookbook*. Your encouragement, advice, and support made doing this second book even more exciting than the first and helped us to improve all of our methods, recipes, and techniques.

These little blurbs can't possibly do justice to each of the people who have dedicated so much time, creativity, and support to this amazing project, but I will try my best. Thank you to:

* Stacey Glick, my wonderful literary agent, who has shown me so much personal support and also understands my crazy schedule. Your guidance is invaluable, and your art of communication is something every author should have.

* Christie Matheson, my amazing coauthor, friend, and confidante. How do I do anything without asking your opinion first? Once again you have made what

could have been a painful process absolutely seamless. Your creative ideas and constant encouragement are rare gifts that complement your outstanding sense of style and organizational abilities. Thank you for always believing in Confetti Cakes and for still acting surprised when we create something great!

* Ben Fink, the remarkable photographer who brought the cakes to life and whose detailed images give readers amazing guidance. We are eternally grateful for your patience and understanding and could not have picked a better match for this project. Thank you for all the beautiful images!

* Gary Tooth, our outstanding graphic designer. We could not have imagined anyone else doing this job. Your concept for this book was exactly what I was dreaming of without ever talking about it! Thanks to both you and Eileen Baumgartner for giving our book the look and style we desired. Your genius and expertise are matched only by your dedication to every project you take on.

This book would not exist without the entire team at Little, Brown:

* Tracy Behar, our meticulous editor. Thank you for your encouragement and support from the very beginning of this project. Your suggestions and ideas were invaluable.

* Brooke Stetson. Thanks for assisting Tracy and Confetti Cakes on all the important details that make our book so special.

* Heather Fain and Carolyn O'Keefe. Thanks for being such attentive and supportive publicists.

* Peggy Freudenthal, for leading the copy editing team, and Marie Salter, for giving the manuscript such care and attention.

My heartfelt thanks goes to the gang at the bakery:

* Candice Corbin, my magnificent assistant, who cares so much and whose opinion I could not value more. Your fantastic ability to handle all the

demands of Confetti Cakes is a source of constant wonderment to me, and I am thankful for you every day.

* Mark Randazzo. More then anyone else, your hands are in the details of this book. Your precision and your patience with the process were unwavering. You made a positive impression on everyone who passed through the bakery during your time here. I could not have asked for a greater collaborator, and I wish you all the best with Mark Joseph Cakes.

* Amanda Waters, my superb bakery assistant. You have incredible talent and have brought your kind heart, skilled hands, and artistic eye to us. We are all so grateful you have joined our family.

Additionally, there are a number of people that have helped to make my job much easier when I am not making cakes and have to run a business. Thank you to:

* All the "girls" at Sarah Hall Productions, for your tireless effort in promoting our first book.

* Kristin Schreiber and Edward Stern, for always getting me out of a computer crisis.

* Allison Lucas and Alan Franklin, for brilliant legal guidance.

* Jeff Googel, for always believing in me.

* William Faivus, for your unending patience with our multitudes of questions.

* The faculty and students at the Institute for Culinary Education and the French Culinary Institute, for your confidence and invaluable support.

I cannot even begin to thank everyone who deserves a hug from me.

My friends and family — including my brother, cousins, aunts and uncles — and my fabulous clients and students all have given me so much love and support I do not know what I would do with out them. Thank you for coming to book signings, sending notes of encouragement, and above all for showing me that you care. I hope you each know how much I value you.

My parents are in everything I do. Thank you for your unwavering support, guidance, and love.

And, most of all, thank you to my husband, Marc. Each day is amazing because I have a chance to spend it with you.

Index